Simply Natural

SIMPLY NATURAL

ALL-TIME *Favorite Recipes*
from the Kitchens *of* North
America's *Best* Natural Foods
RESTAURANTS

LES SUSSMAN & SALLY BORDWELL

NEW WORLD LIBRARY
NOVATO, CALIFORNIA

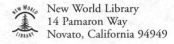 New World Library
14 Pamaron Way
Novato, California 94949

Cover art and design by Kathy Warinner
Text design and layout by Aaron Kenedi
Production by Mary Ann Casler

Library of Congress Cataloging-in-Publication Data
Sussman, Les, 1944–
    Simply Natural: all-time favorite recipes from the kitchens of North America's best natural foods restaurants / Les Sussman & Sally Bordwell.
        p.   cm.
    Includes index.
    ISBN 1-57731-020-9 (alk. paper)
    1. Cookery (Natural Foods) 2. Vegetarian Cookery. 3. Natural food restaurants—United States—Guide books. 4. Natural food restaurants—Canada—Guidebooks. 5. Vegetarian restaurants—United States—Guidebooks. 6. Vegetarian restaurants—Canada—Guidebooks.

    I. Bordwell, Sally, 1947–   .   II. Title.
    TX741.S87   1998
    641.5'63—dc21   98-46531
                                                                            CIP

First printing, November 1998
ISBN 1-57731-020-9
Printed in Canada on acid-free paper
Distributed to the trade by Publishers Group West
10 9 8 7 6 5 4 3 2 1

To everyone who believes in the sanctity of all life

Contents

Acknowledgments

This book is much like an elaborate recipe: A lot of ingredients went into its preparation.

The most basic ingredients were the many food writers and editors of newspapers and magazines across the country who gave us their enthusiastic assistance, as well as members of various vegetarian organizations stretching from coast to coast.

Although space prohibits us from thanking everyone who helped, we would like to extend special appreciation to the following people:

Jean Wolinsky, publicist with the James Beard Foundation; the staff at Gulliver's, New York City's primo vegetarian cooking school; Christiana Meunier, publisher and editor of *Vegetarian Gourmet* magazine; Sharon Lane, food editor, *Seattle Times;* Jeanne Rosen Brown, food editor, *Chicago Tribune;* Elizabeth Black, food editor of the *New York Daily News;* and Kathy Foster, food writer, *Miami Herald.*

We are also indebted to the following publications for their assistance: *Boston Magazine*; *Chicago Reader, Chicago-Sun Times, Denver Post, Jersey Journal, Macro Chef Magazine, Memphis Magazine, Nashville Banner, New York Post, Palm Springs Life Magazine, Salt Lake*

City Magazine, Vegetarian Journal, Vegetarian Singles News, and *Zagat Survey.*

Special thanks go to these vegetarian organizations: Vegetarian Awareness Network, Vegetarian Resource Group, Vegetarian Information Service, Vegetarian Society of D.C., EarthSave, Vegetarian Society of Colorado, Vegetarian Society of Houston, Vegetarian Society of New York, Vancouver Island Vegetarian Association, and the Toronto Vegetarian Association.

Thanks also to Munro Magruder, marketing and subsidiary rights director at New World Library, who was enthusiastic about this book idea; Becky Benenate, Jason Gardner, and Tona Pearce Myers, our hard-working editors; and our literary agent and dear friend, Claire Gerus.

Last but not least, we owe a great debt of gratitude to Jennifer Doctorow, who did much of the research. Without Jennifer's untiring assistance, this book could not have been completed.

Across the border, thanks to our Canadian researcher, Scott Gerus.

Introduction

Welcome to an excursion into the world of healthful natural foods dining — one that will help you feel better, look younger, and maybe even live longer.

Whether you are new to the tantalizing delights of natural foods or a life-long devotee, this book will whet your appetite with some of the best recipes from top natural foods restaurants in the United States and Canada.

And just in case you're feeling a bit too lazy to slave over a hot stove, you can use this book as a handy guide to locating and learning about the restaurants whose recipes appear here. Eating a healthy meal at one of these many interesting restaurants can be just as much fun as preparing their delicious meals at home.

This book is the result of hundreds of letters and questionnaires sent to restaurant owners throughout North America and Canada — and almost an equal number of telephone conversations. At last count, there were more than 2,000 natural foods restaurants in operation throughout North America, and our goal was to ferret out the best.

In order to find the best natural foods restaurants, in addition to researching various periodicals we also consulted with food editors and writers at major newspapers and magazines from Manhattan to Montreal.

Additionally, we contacted prominent vegetarian organizations, such as the Vegetarian Resource Group and the Vegetarian Information Service, seeking their recommendations for restaurants to be included in this book.

Also helpful in our research were such popular dining guides as the *Zagat Survey* and the *Vegetarian Journal's Guide to Natural Foods Restaurants*. Once we assembled our list, we contacted the restaurant owners and asked them three questions: what their establishment's most popular dish was, why that was so, and how to prepare that dish at home.

Because we wanted this book to be used as a travel guide for the health-conscious traveler, as well as a cookbook, we also asked owners to provide us with a description of the restaurant's decor, and to tell us anything interesting about its location and the types of people who dined there — whether it was a student crowd, filled with locals, or touristy.

While some states are omitted — sometimes because we couldn't find any natural foods eateries worthy of recommendation, or simply because restaurant owners failed to respond to our questionnaire — you will nonetheless find in these pages a useful, comprehensive guide to health-conscious restaurants, the varieties of cuisine they serve, and their most popular dishes.

You will also be provided with information about which of these restaurants take credit cards, serve alcohol, and allow smoking, and whether or not they are wheelchair accessible.

With this book as your cookbook and travel guide, you'll be treated to cuisine that's as imaginative and diverse as the American people. You will discover unique hole-in-the-wall cafes in rural areas serving top-notch natural foods, and elegant urban restaurants that prepare world-class gourmet vegetarian cuisine.

And you will also have at your fingertips sumptuous recipes that are easy to prepare at home — everything from breakfasts and appetizers to main entrées and desserts.

The criterion for inclusion in this book — besides reputation — was that the restaurant be either completely vegetarian, vegan (no type of animal food, dairy, eggs, or honey used to prepare the food), macrobiotic (mostly vegan, with some fish dishes), or offer a good number of vegetarian dishes along with its regular menu.

Please keep in mind when reading this book that there is a big difference between natural foods restaurants — the category in which all of these restaurants fit — and strictly vegetarian or vegan restaurants. Many natural foods restaurants cater to a wider spectrum of appetites and also serve some poultry, fish, and in a few cases, red meat. Vegetarian and vegan-oriented establishments, on the other hand, do not.

While we believe that a vegetarian diet is the moral and ethical way to eat — as well as being the best road toward better health — we did not want to eliminate restaurants whose chefs are doing their best to prepare sumptuous haute vegetarian cuisine simply because they are also catering to the tastes of what we feel are dwindling numbers of nonvegetarians.

What we hope, most of all, is that you, your family, and friends will enjoy these tempting recipes — many of them low in fat — and that if you like this approach to dining, that you spread the word about the pleasures of a natural foods diet.

To your health, vitality, and energy.

Glossary

Agar agar: A white gelatinous substance derived from a sea vegetable and used as a gelatin base.

Arame: A thin and threadlike dark brown sea vegetable. Rich in iron, calcium, and other minerals, it is often served as a side dish.

Azuki: Small dark red beans.

Brown rice: Unpolished rice that has had only its tough, outer husk removed.

Burdock: A wild plant that grows throughout the United States. Its root is highly valued in macrobiotic cooking for its strength-giving properties.

Daikon: A long, mild white Japanese radish.

Dashi: A traditional Japanese broth made from shoyu, kombu, shiitake mushrooms, and fresh ginger.

Kombu: A wide, thick, dark green sea vegetable that is rich in minerals.

Kudzu: Made from the root of a wild vine, this white starch is used for thickening sauces.

Lacto-vegetarian: A vegetarian who abstains from eggs as well as meat, but consumes milk products.

Lacto-ovo vegetarian: A vegetarian who consumes both eggs and milk products, although avoiding flesh foods.

Macrobiotic: An eating style based on the Asian principles of yin and yang (masculine and feminine). It is primarily vegan, but some fish is utilized.

Millet: A fluffy whole grain used in soups, vegetable dishes, casseroles, and as a cereal.

Mirin: A sweet cooking wine made from sweet rice.

Miso: A fermented paste made from soybeans, sea salt, and usually rice and barley. It is used in soup stocks and as a seasoning.

Nori: Thin sheets of dried sea vegetable.

Norimaki: Rice, vegetables, and condiments wrapped in a roasted nori sheet; it's served sushi style, in sliced rounds.

Organic: Farming methods that work in harmony with nature and use no toxic chemicals.

Paneer: A mild Indian cheese made with cow's milk.

Sea salt: Salt obtained from evaporated sea water.

Seitan: *See* wheat gluten.

Shiitake: A delicious mushroom used fresh or dried.

Shoyu: The naturally fermented Asian seasoning made from whole wheat, soybeans, salt, water, and wheat koji — known popularly as soy sauce.

Soba: Asian noodles made from buckwheat flour or buckwheat, combined with whole wheat.

Spelt: People who are sensitive to wheat usually are able to tolerate this ancestor of contemporary grains of wheat.

Tahini: Sesame paste.

Tamari soy sauce: A dark soy sauce that is slightly thicker than shoyu.

Tempeh: A pressed fermented-soybean cake. High in protein, it is eaten in Indonesia and Sri Lanka as a staple food.

Tofu: A protein-rich soybean curd that is used in dressings, soups, and vegetable dishes.

Udon: Japanese-style noodles made from whole wheat, or whole wheat and unbleached white flour.

Umeboshi: A salted, pickled plum that stimulates the appetite and digestion. Available whole or in paste form.

Vegan: Pronounced *vee-gan*, this term refers to vegetarians who refuse to eat (or use) any animal products, including milk, cheese, other dairy foods, eggs, wool, silk, suede, or leather.

Vegetarian: Anyone who refrains from eating meat, fish, and poultry.

Wakame: A long, thin green sea vegetable with a sweet taste and delicate texture.

Wasabi: A Japanese horseradish, light green in color.

Wheat gluten: This is also called seitan. Made from wheat, with the texture of meat.

LEGEND

Price of Entrées
Inexpensive: less than $7.00
Moderate: $7.00 to $15.00
Expensive: more than $15.00

Credit Cards
AE: American Express
D: Discover
DC: Diner's Club
MC: Mastercard
V: Visa

GOLDEN TEMPLE NATURAL GROCERY AND CAFE
1901 Eleventh Avenue South
Birmingham, Alabama 35205
205-933-6333

OPEN MONDAY THROUGH FRIDAY 8:30 A.M. TO 7 P.M., SATURDAY 9:30 A.M. TO 5:30 P.M., SUNDAY NOON TO 5:30 P.M.

Price: Inexpensive
Credit cards: MC, V
Wheelchair accessible
No smoking
No alcohol

Owner Harinam Khalsa credits the success of his "pure" vegetarian restaurant with being in the right place at the right time. He explains that the cafe, located in an old building, has not changed much in the more than two decades since he first opened his doors, although the neighborhood certainly has.

The neighborhood near the University of Alabama was once on the shabby side, he notes. Over the years, however, shabby turned into Birmingham's trendy entertainment mecca. As a result, the Golden Temple struck gold and sometimes found it difficult keeping up with the increased numbers of customers who began flocking to the area.

For people-watching, the restaurant's sidewalk seating is ideal. If it's quiet conversation you desire, simply step inside. Here you will find a casual, warm, and quiet atmosphere, replete with wooden tables and lunch counter.

There are plenty of plants everywhere, giving the restaurant a rain forest look. There is also an open kitchen, so people can watch their food being made.

This natural foods restaurant and grocery store, open only for lunch, features dairy-free vegetarian cuisine. Organic products are used whenever possible. Light food is the aim here, and most dishes have fewer than 5 grams of fat.

Specials include Monday Vegetable Curry (lentils, chickpeas, tofu, cauliflower, potatoes, and chutney) and a popular Thursday dish called Southern Soul Food (black-eyed peas, sweet potatoes, collard greens, and corn on the cob).

Another best-seller and a regular menu item is the Black Bean Burrito (black beans with Monterey jack cheese, wrapped in a whole-wheat yeast-free chapati and grilled, topped with salsa, sour cream, and jalapenos, and served with a side of rice).

Also a favorite is Quesadillas (black beans, bell peppers, onions, green chilies, mushrooms, and shredded Monterey jack cheese, layered and grilled between chapatis and topped with salsa, sour cream, guacamole, and jalapenos).

For university students (and anyone else) on a tight budget, the soup of the day, which comes with whole-grain bread, is a popular choice; a second serving is half the price of the first. Drinks include a choice of fresh vegetable juices as well as various sodas and water. Herbal teas and organic coffees are also available.

Lasagna

Serves 6 to 8 as a main course

Catherine Cocke, the restaurant's assistant manager, picks lasagna as one of the Golden Temple's most popular dishes because "it's a wonderful-tasting dish that's easy to make at home. I think you'll find it just as popular with your guests as with ours.

"Eggplant Parmesan is another of the cafe's popular specials on Italian Cuisine Day. It seems to disappear as quickly as we prepare it."

TOMATO SAUCE
Olive oil or water
1 cup finely chopped onions
6 ounces white mushrooms, sliced
1 green bell pepper, seeded, deribbed, and finely diced
3 cups crushed tomatoes
1 cup water
2 to 3 tablespoons dried basil
2 to 3 teaspoons dried oregano
3 tablespoons fresh parsley, minced
Pinch of dried sage
Pinch of dried rosemary
Pinch of red pepper flakes
Salt and freshly ground pepper to taste
Tamari soy sauce to taste

8 ounces dried whole-wheat or artichoke lasagna noodles
3/4 cup cottage cheese
$1^1/2$ cups ricotta cheese
1 cup shredded sharp Cheddar cheese
Grated Romano cheese

To make sauce: In a large, heavy saucepan, heat oil or water over medium heat and sauté onions, mushrooms, and pepper until onions are translucent and peppers are al dente. Add tomatoes, water, herbs, and pepper flakes. Cover and simmer for 30 minutes.

In a large pot of salted boiling water, cook pasta until al dente, 8 to 10 minutes. Drain.

Preheat oven to 400ºF. Spread a light layer of the tomato sauce in a baking dish. Place one layer of noodles in dish. Spread with $^1/3$ of the sauce, then with $^1/3$ of the cottage cheese and ricotta cheese mixed together. Add another layer of noodles, sauce, Cheddar, and a sprinkle of Romano. Add remaining noodles, sauce, and another sprinkle of Romano.

Bake for about 1 hour, or until golden brown. Let sit for 15 minutes before cutting.

Eggplant Parmesan

Serves 4 as a main course

3 to 4 globe eggplants, peeled
Tomato Sauce (page 11)
1 cup shredded Cheddar
$^1/2$ cup mozzarella cheese
Grated Romano cheese

Preheat oven to 400ºF.

Cut eggplants into 5/8-inch-thin crosswise slices. Soak in salted water for 5 minutes. Drain. Steam over boiling water in a covered pot for 10 minutes or until al dente.

In the bottom of a baking dish spread a layer of tomato sauce. Add a layer of half of eggplant, half of remaining sauce, a layer of half the Cheddar and mozzarella, and a sprinkle of the Romano. Repeat, ending with a layer of Cheddar or mozzarella, and a sprinkle of Romano.

Bake until bubbly, about 20 minutes. Add another sprinkle of Romano and bake for 10 minutes.

GENTLE STRENGTH COOPERATIVE
234 West University Drive
Tempe, Arizona 85281
602-968-4831

Price: Inexpensive
Credit cards: MC, V
Wheelchair accessible
No smoking
No alcohol

Tucked behind a berm spilling over with wildflowers in the middle of concrete highways and parking lots in downtown Tempe is the Gentle Strength Cooperative.

It's a natural foods grocery store and deli where you will find an eclectic mix of students, professors from nearby Arizona State University, co-op members, business professionals, and travelers.

The deli features patio dining where customers can eat alfresco "100 percent organic vegetarian delights that are prepared from scratch." Gentle Strength offers macrobiotic meals, salads, hot and cold entrées, gourmet vegan desserts — including award-winning muffins — and their signature salsas and salad dressings.

Among the most popular dishes are the Organic Stir-Fry with Buckwheat Udon Noodles, the Garden Focaccia Sandwich, and macrobiotic specialties.

Bodacious Bialy

Serves 1 to 2

Gentle Strength selected the Bodacious Bialy "because it is a popular sandwich with our clientele. The sandwich is a main meal that embodies the spirit of the co-op. It is fresh, organic, with a variety of textures and tastes.

"The recipe is easy to prepare and perfect for dining alfresco, which is very popular in Tempe. Each day on our patio you will find our customers enjoying a Bodacious Bialy or any of our other fresh organic menu items."

BASIL-TOFU SPREAD
3/4 cup packed fresh basil leaves
1/4 cup sun-dried tomatoes
1 tablespoon minced garlic
1/4 cup grated Parmesan cheese
2 tablespoons olive oil
2 cups firm silken tofu

1 plain or onion bialy (A bialy is a bagel-shaped bread with an onion center. It can
    be toasted if desired.)
2 thin slices of tomato
Sunflower sprouts, mixed salad greens, and whole fresh basil leaves for serving

To make spread: In a blender, combine all ingredients and puree until smooth. Cut bialy in half and coat both halves with basil-tofu spread. Add tomato, sunflower sprouts, greens, and basil leaves to one half and top with other half.

DAIRY HOLLOW HOUSE
515 Spring Street
Eureka Springs, Arkansas 72632
501-253-7444

OPEN FOR DINNER (TO GUESTS NOT STAYING AT THE INN) ON SPECIAL OCCASIONS, SUCH AS THANKSGIVING AND ABOUT TWELVE PRE-ARRANGED AND ADVERTISED EVENINGS. CALL FOR INFORMATION. OPEN FOR DINNER DAILY FOR INN GUESTS.

Price: Expensive
All major credit cards
Wheelchair accessible
No smoking
Alcohol: BYO

This elegant, romantic, and award-winning country inn and restaurant is snuggled in the Ozark Mountain resort town of Eureka Springs, just a mile from the historic downtown area.

The inn and restaurant is famous for its rustic charm, friendly and attentive owners and staff, luxurious attention to the details of guests' comfort, and — especially — its amazing food.

Since 1995, the restaurant has no longer offered nightly dinners, opting instead for "pull-out-all-the-stops feasts" for special occasions: sumptuous meals made from scratch with seasonal and regional ingredients that will satisfy vegetarians and nonvegetarians alike.

The restaurant, which has been applauded by publications ranging from *USA Today* to *Glamour* magazine, is operated by Ned Shank and Crescent Dragonwagon, who also serves as the inn's chef and is a cookbook author.

Ned offers the following glowing description of the restaurant: "The dining room is a light, flower-filled, airy room with vaulted ceilings and numerous lace-covered windows looking out onto the park behind. The walls in the dining room have a twig lattice wainscoting with a soft floral fabric backing.

"The walls above the lattice are painted a creamy white. A twig picture-rail circles the room below the ceiling, and is intertwined with an ivy stencil. The wall above the picture rail and the ceiling are painted a pale yellow.

"A massive stone fireplace is centered on one wall with a mantel topped by a thick slab of polished cedar, and hanging from one wall is a large handmade art quilt called 'Tea with Aunt Rose,' by *Dairy Hollow House Cookbook* coauthor Jan Brown." (The quilt went with Crescent and Ned when they served a thousand-guest brunch at President Clinton's first inaugural.)

If you want to spend the night, accommodations are in two homes on either side of a peaceful, wooded green valley. Choose the Farmhouse or the Main House; each has its own magic.

Deep December Ragout of Seitan, Shiitakes, and Winter Vegetables with Garlic and Red Wine

Serves 4 to 6 as a main course

Chef, innkeeper, and cookbook author Crescent Dragonwagon describes Deep December Ragout as a longtime restaurant favorite. "This stew is hearty, deeply flavorful, lapped in a rich, glossy, savory sauce, and spiked with red wine. It's serious wintertime satisfaction in a bowl.

"This is everything you want from a stew, from the seductive aroma with which it warms the house as it simmers, to its robust, filling substance and big, distinct chunks of potato and other vegetables.

"Although the ragout is everything you want, it's nothing you don't want: no fatty layer requiring degreasing, no stew beef cooked past flavor and recognition to mere stringiness.

"And though it is absolutely *impossible* that something so stalwart should be low-fat, low-fat it is. You can serve it in a bowl, accompanied with a hunk of good bread, and start if off with a big green salad splashed with a tart vinaigrette or nonsweet sesame dressing.

"Or try it ladled over any cooked grain or pasta. In any case, you'll have a wafting fragrance in the house presaging the most fulfilling of cold-weather meals — a combination guaranteed to console the disheartened and nourish the dispirited."

1 tablespoon olive oil

1 large onion, cut vertically into crescent-shaped slivers

1/4 cup unbleached all-purpose flour

3 1/2 cups vegetable stock

1/4 cup nutritional yeast

1/4 cup tamari soy sauce

1 cup hearty, full-bodied, tannic red wine, such as Cabernet, Barolo, or Barbaresco

1 tablespoon umeboshi vinegar

1 tablespoon honey

Major grinding of black pepper — 1/2 to 1 teaspoon or so

1 cup canned diced tomatoes in tomato puree

8 to 10 garlic cloves, quartered or thickly sliced

1/4 teaspoon salt

1/8 teaspoon cayenne pepper

6 to 8 dried shiitake mushrooms, broken roughly into quarters

One 8-ounce package seitan, well drained and cut into 1-inch cubes

4 small unpeeled potatoes, scrubbed and cut into large pieces

2 unpeeled carrots, scrubbed and cut into 1/2-inch-thick rounds

1 parsnip, halved lengthwise and cut into 1/2-inch half-rounds

8 ounces green beans, trimmed and cut into 3-inch-long pieces (2 cups)

1 zucchini, halved lengthwise and cut into 1/2-inch-thick half-rounds

Minced fresh flat-leaf parsley for garnish (optional)

Spray Dutch oven with vegetable oil cooking spray or use a nonstick pan. Over medium-high heat, heat oil and sauté the onion for about 6 minutes, or until pieces start to brown.

Sprinkle onion with flour, reduce heat to medium, and cook for about 4 minutes. Stir in $1/2$ cup vegetable stock until blended. Stir in a little more stock, then remaining amount. Add yeast (you will think it's going to lump, but the flakes will dissolve), soy sauce, red wine, vinegar, honey, pepper, tomatoes, garlic, salt, and cayenne. Bring to a boil, then reduce heat to a simmer.

Drop in mushrooms (they will hydrate as stew cooks), with seitan, potatoes, carrots, parsnip, and green beans. Reduce heat, cover, and barely simmer, stirring every so often, for 35 minutes, or until potatoes are nearly done. Lift lid, drop in zucchini, re-cover, and let cook another 10 to 15 minutes more, or until vegetables are tender but not mushy. Serve hot, with a sprinkle of parsley, if you like.

Oven Roasted Shiitake Mushrooms with Garlic and Coarse Salt

Serves 6 to 8 as an appetizer

Crescent says that this recipe is so good, "it'll make you want to stand on your tail, clap your flippers, and bark like a seal. This is much loved at the restaurant."

$1^{1}/4$ pounds shiitake mushrooms, stemmed
2 to 4 tablespoons olive oil (see note)
$1^{1}/2$ tablespoons finely minced garlic
$1^{1}/2$ teaspoons coarse sea salt (if salt is in very large crystals, you may crush it a
        bit in a mortar and pestle)
Fresh herb sprigs for garnish (optional)

Preheat oven to 400°F. Choose a baking dish large enough to hold all mushrooms in one layer. Spray dish with vegetable-oil cooking spray. Place mushrooms in dish.

Toss mushrooms with oil, garlic, and salt. Bake uncovered for 10 minutes. Remove from oven and shake pan a few times. Some mushrooms should be starting to get a little golden on the underneath side of caps. Bake until at least a third of the mushrooms are starting to color, 3 to 5 minutes. With the lesser amount of oil, this happens more quickly.

Serve warm or at room temperature garnished with herb sprigs, if you like.

NOTE: LESS OIL YIELDS MUSHROOMS THAT ARE DRIER AROUND THE EDGES; MORE OIL YIELDS MORE SUCCULENT, MOISTER MUSHROOMS.

Oatmeal-Cornmeal Blueberry Bread

Makes 1 large, 2 medium, or 3 mini-loaves

Crescent offers this dish as a "breakfast basket favorite" at the inn between June and July. "We make it just in time for fresh blueberries! It's a perfect, not-too-sweet bread that is great for tea, breakfast — maybe even dessert.

"Cornmeal gives a pleasant toothy crunch, lemon a subtle accent; the blueberries are little explosions of color and flavor in the pale golden loaf. Its texture is light, firm, reminiscent of pound cake, yet it's very low in fat."

1 1/2 cups unbleached all-purpose flour
1/3 cup stone-ground yellow cornmeal
1/2 teaspoon baking soda
1 teaspoon baking powder

^{1}/2 teaspoon salt

1 cup fresh blueberries, washed and picked over, or thawed frozen blueberries

^{1}/4 cup old-fashioned rolled oats

2 to 4 tablespoons walnuts, toasted and chopped (optional)

3 tablespoons mild oil, such as corn, canola, or peanut

2 eggs

^{1}/2 cup plus 2 tablespoons buttermilk

^{3}/4 cup sugar

Finely grated zest of 1 lemon

Preheat oven to 350ºF. Coat 1 large, 2 medium, or 3 small loaf pans with vegetable-oil cooking spray. Sift the flour, cornmeal, baking soda, baking powder, and salt together into a large bowl.

In a small bowl, combine the blueberries, oats, and optional walnuts, and sprinkle 1 tablespoon of flour mixture over them.

In a medium bowl, beat oil, eggs, buttermilk, sugar, and zest together.

Stir the wet mixture into the dry mixture using as few strokes as possible. Gently stir in the blueberry mixture to make a stiff batter.

Spoon batter into prepared pan(s). Bake until lightly browned, 45 to 55 minutes for large loaf, 35 to 50 minutes for medium loaves, and 35 to 40 for small loaves. Check two-thirds of the way through the baking period; if loaves are browning excessively, tent loosely with aluminum foil.

Let breads cool 10 minutes in pan, then run a knife around the edges of the pan(s), and turn loaves out on a wire rack to cool completely.

Sandy's Great Lentil Soup with Greens

Serves 4 to 6 as an appetizer

Sometimes — especially after all the rich food of the holidays — simple is best. Crescent says, "This great, easy, healthy, homey lentil soup developed by kitchen manager Sandy Allison can't be beat. The few ingredients belie its deliciousness.

"The garlic and olive oil give a rich, almost meaty taste, yet it is vegetarian and tastes even better the next day. It is based on a recipe given Sandy by Markita Sorce, another fine local cook."

2 tablespoons to $1/2$ cup olive oil

2 large onions, diced

$2^1/2$ cups dried green lentils

About 8 cups water

2 teaspoons cumin seeds

Salt and freshly ground pepper to taste

1 head fresh garlic, separated into cloves and peeled

1 to $1^1/2$ pounds fresh greens (spinach, collard, turnip, etc.; a combination is best), well washed, stemmed, and chopped

Plain yogurt or sour cream, homemade salsa, and minced fresh cilantro for garnish (optional)

Spray a medium skillet with vegetable-oil cooking spray. Heat oil (more is tastier; less is saner in terms of fat grams) over medium heat and sauté onions until very soft.

Transfer onions to a soup pot and add lentils and water. Bring to a boil, reduce heat to a simmer, cover, and cook until lentils are soft — about 1 hour.

Add cumin, salt, and pepper. Scoop out a ladleful of soup and puree it in a blender with garlic. Return lentil puree to soup. Bring to a boil, drop in greens, partially cover, and simmer for 10 to 15 minutes.

Taste and correct seasoning. Garnish with a dab of yogurt or sour cream, some salsa, and some cilantro, if you like.

FLEA STREET CAFE
3607 Alameda de las Pulgas
Menlo Park, California 94025
650-854-1226

OPEN FOR LUNCH TUESDAY THROUGH FRIDAY 11:30 A.M. TO 2 P.M.; DINNER TUESDAY THROUGH FRIDAY 5:30 TO 9:30 P.M.; BRUNCH SUNDAY 10 A.M. TO 2 P.M.

Price: Expensive
Credit cards: AE, MC, V
Wheelchair accessible
No smoking
Alcohol: Extensive wine list
featuring many local wines

Chef/owner and accomplished cookbook author Jesse Cool admits that she's downright fanatical about her produce.

Part of the original wave of California chefs to concentrate on local, seasonally grown, and organic ingredients, Flea Street's kitchen searches the season's most interesting produce, which is scattered throughout her menu.

As a result, the food is robustly seasoned and beautiful to look at because of its freshness. The salad greens and vegetables served here, for example, are grown by a local farmer who has been supplying the cafe for more than 10 years.

The casual but elegant restaurant's decor is beautiful to look at as well, with what Jesse describes as a "gentle, European country inn feel."

A series of dining rooms are appointed with antiques, flowers, and personal art. Other decorative elements include cabbage-rose wallpaper, raspberry sherbet-colored walls, and antique plates. Lace-curtained windows divide the rooms, and the tables are set with unmatched floral dishes.

The Flea Street Cafe always offers vegetarian options, with plenty of options for vegans. "Our food is real, local when possible, and grown with care," Jesse notes. "We use organic butter, olive oil, coffee, and as much organic everything else as is possible."

Among the popular specials are the Seasonal Farmer's Pie, a puff pastry shell filled with garlic mashed potatoes and surrounded by an array of grilled, roasted, and steamed local vegetables. Also a favorite is Green Onion Noodle Cake with shiitake mushrooms and rock shrimp in a Thai chili sauce.

The fresh fish of the day might be locally caught halibut with olive oil, lemon zest, and oregano, then topped with mounds of marinated multicolored tomatoes, Greek olives, and feta cheese and served over roasted eggplant, or wild Half Moon Bay Salmon over Chived Mashed Potatoes, served with seasonal vegetables.

Always in demand is the Wild, Wild Pasta (fettuccine with wild mushrooms, wild rice, sun-dried tomatoes, and feta cheese in an olive oil, oregano, and garlic sauce).

Range-free and hormone-free chicken and some meat dishes are also found on the menu. For dessert, a favorite is the angel food cake garnished with rose petals and lavender from the restaurant's own garden and topped with berries. Other in-demand desserts include old fashioned chocolate cake with figs dipped in warm fudge sauce, and seasonal sorbets such as huckleberry cantaloupe.

Zucchini Pancakes with Golden Tomato Concassé

Makes 8 to 10 pancakes, serves 4 to 5 as a main course

This recipe and the one that follows appear in Jesse Cool's cookbook, *Tomatoes: A Country Garden Cookbook* (Collins Publishers). She describes the Zucchini Pancakes with Golden Tomato Concassé as a recipe "perfect for those times in late summer when it seems like everybody's neighbor is giving away oversized zucchini and handfuls of very ripe tomatoes.

"This recipe utilizes them both. The zucchini pancakes are light, but watch out! It's easy to eat too many."

1 pound golden tomatoes, peeled, seeded, and coarsely chopped
$1^1/2$ pounds zucchini or other summer squash
1 medium red onion
$1^1/2$ teaspoons salt
1 garlic clove, crushed
2 tablespoons minced fresh mint or basil
$1/8$ teaspoon ground nutmeg
2 tablespoons grated Parmesan cheese
1 large egg, beaten
3 tablespoons unbleached all-purpose flour
Salt and freshly ground black pepper to taste
Light olive oil or canola oil for frying

Place tomatoes in a colander set over a bowl and drain, saving juices for future use. Set aside.

Grate zucchini and onion into a bowl and sprinkle with salt. Let stand for 10 minutes, then squeeze out any excess water. Combine with all remaining ingredients except oil and tomatoes.

In a large heavy skillet, over medium heat, heat $1/4$ inch oil until almost smoking. Drop $1/4$-

cup portions of zucchini batter into hot oil. Flatten if necessary. Let pancake completely brown on one side before flipping to brown other side.

Transfer tomatoes from colander to a bowl. Salt and pepper them. Serve tomato concassé on top of or under pancakes.

Fresh Pasta with Just-Warmed Tomato Sauce

Serves 4 as a main course

"This tomato sauce recipe is so easy it is embarrassing," says Jesse. "It's a reminder of how good food can be without much effort. In fact, it takes more time to make the pasta. The tomatoes must be vine-ripened tomatoes at the peak of flavor for the finished dish to be the same. If you're pinched for time, purchase 1 pound fresh fettuccine, but don't skimp on the sauce."

FRESH PASTA
4 cups unbleached white flour
1 teaspoon salt
4 eggs
1 to 2 teaspoons water or until dough comes together

TOMATO SAUCE
$1/3$ cup virgin olive oil
1 small yellow onion, thinly sliced
3 garlic cloves, minced
$1/2$ cup dry red wine
1 tablespoon coarsely chopped fresh oregano
$1/2$ cup coarsely chopped fresh parsley or basil

2 pounds ripe tomatoes, peeled, chopped, and seeded juices reserved
Salt and add freshly ground pepper to taste

To make pasta: In a large bowl or on a large, flat surface, combine flour and salt. Make a well in center of flour mixture. Using your hands, gently blend flour and eggs together. Add just enough water to form a stiff dough. Knead on a lightly floured board for about 10 minutes to form a smooth, elastic dough. Cover and let sit for about 30 minutes.

Using a pasta machine, roll dough very thin and hand cut into 1-inch strips. Toss pasta in extra flour to prevent them from sticking together.

To make sauce: In a large heavy saucepan, over medium heat, heat oil and sauté onion and garlic for about 5 minutes. Add red wine and herbs, stir, and cook for 3 to 4 minutes.

Turn off heat and add tomatoes to pan. Toss and season with salt and pepper. Add reserved tomato juice or a bit of water to create a thinner sauce if you choose.

In a large pot of salted boiling water, cook pasta until al dente, 2 to 3 minutes. Toss with tomato sauce and serve on a large platter.

For a Mexican touch, try garnishing the noodles with avocado slices, crumbled queso fresco or shredded jack cheese, and chopped cilantro.

FOLLOW YOUR HEART NATURAL FOODS MARKET AND CAFE
21825 Sherman Way
Canoga Park, California 91303
818-348-3240

OPEN DAILY 8 A.M. TO 9 P.M.

Price: Inexpensive to moderate
Credit cards: MC, V
Wheelchair accessible
No smoking
No alcohol

"There's much more to this restaurant than the name implies," enthuses owner Mary Paterson. "Yes, you'll find aisles filled with natural foods groceries, vitamins, herbs, and delicious deli goods — but there's more to it. We're known far and wide as one of the finest vegetarian restaurants in California."

Started in 1971 by four friends who pooled their limited resources to open a soup and sandwich shop, this classic natural foods restaurant has been voted one of the eight best restaurants in California by the Vegetarian Resource Group, a nationwide clearing house on vegetarian lifestyles.

The cafe is tucked away in the back of the market, and has a casual decor. For diners who enjoy fresh air, there is outdoor patio seating. For singles, the counter located inside the restaurant is highly recommended. "The counter is a unique part of the cafe experience," Paterson says. "Many friendships have begun as a result of a chance encounter there."

The clientele here is eclectic. They range from sixties hippies, aerospace engineers, and corporate executives to entire families and creative types including, at times, some well-known Hollywood faces.

Besides the hearty comradeship here, you will also find hearty portions of great-tasting vegetarian dishes. In addition to the standard menu, the cafe's chefs always seem to be coming up with something new.

Favorites include the cafe's legendary homemade soups and the Nutburger (a nut and vegetable patty on a toasted whole-wheat bun, baked with raw Cheddar cheese and topped with sprouts, tomatoes, pickles, Veganaise, and special sauce) and the Zorro Burrito (black beans, braised tofu, jack and Cheddar cheese, Spanish rice, and salsa wrapped in an over-sized organic whole-wheat tortilla).

Other popular dishes are the Roasted Eggplant, Tomato, and Leek Sandwich and various ethnic specialties that range from enchiladas, wok stir-fries, and pastas to spanakopita. Also on the menu are "three of the best veggie burgers you'll ever chance to eat," Paterson says.

For breakfast aficionados, popular choices include such delicious griddle items as Wheat-Free Cakes (wheatless, dairyless pancakes made with brown rice and other whole grains, with bananas, raspberries, blueberries, and nuts) and Tofu Benedict (poached tofu and tomato on a toasted English muffin smothered in an eggless hollandaise sauce, served with breakfast potatoes, spinach, or vegetarian ham).

Another morning favorite is Two-Bean Hash, served with vegetarian sausage. "Customers in the know often drive the distance just to have this," Paterson says.

Popeye's Swee'pea with Olive Oyl

Serves 8 to 10 as a main course

"We picked this soup recipe because it has been one of our customers' favorites for 25 years," says owner Mary Paterson. "Follow Your Heart has always been known for its delicious, hearty, homemade soups." This soup contains all of Popeye's favorites: peas sweetened with yams ("I yam what I yam"), olive oil, and of course, spinach.

10 cups water

$1^1/2$ pounds dried green split peas ($3^1/4$ cups)

1 large red onion, diced (2 cups)

$1/2$ pounds unpeeled yam, diced (2 cups)

3 large celery stalks

3 tablespoons extra-virgin olive oil

1 pound fresh spinach, washed, stemmed, and finely chopped

2 large garlic cloves, pressed or minced

2 tablespoons minced fresh basil, or 2 teaspoons dried basil

Fresh peas, shelled, or one 10-ounce package frozen peas, rinsed under hot water

3 tablespoons tamari soy sauce

3 tablespoons Barbados or other light molasses, or to taste (do not use blackstrap)

2 teaspoons Spike, or to taste

In a soup pot, combine water, split peas, onion, yam, celery, and olive oil. Bring to a boil, reduce heat to a simmer, cover, and cook for about 30 minutes.

Add spinach, garlic, and basil. Bring to a boil; reduce heat and simmer, covered, 25 to 35 minutes, or until peas have dissolved to form a thick broth. Stir occasionally.

Add fresh or frozen peas and tamari. Add molasses and Spike and simmer for 5 minutes, or until peas are tender and flavors well blended.

INN OF THE SEVENTH RAY
128 Old Topanga Road
Topanga, California 90290
310-455-1311

OPEN DAILY FOR LUNCH 11:30 A.M. TO 2:30 P.M., DINNER 6 TO 10 P.M.

Price: Moderate to expensive
All major credit cards
Wheelchair accessible
No smoking
Alcohol: Beer and wine

Located in the upscale community of Topanga Canyon, Inn of the Seventh Ray is housed in the former Four Square Gospel church, once the hideaway of famed 1930s spiritualist and evangelist Aimee Semple McPherson.

The A-framed church structure still is a hideaway for the many celebrities living in Topanga Canyon who desire privacy when dining out. One of the dining rooms has a wood-burning fireplace, while the other has a clear, Plexiglas roof. But the location of choice is the outside dining area. In fact, the restaurant prides itself on its "outside dining with inside service."

A creek runs along the dining terrace, and patrons are treated to a picturesque view of waterfalls and fountains. Sycamores trees provide shade, and a colorful array of herbs and flowers gently perfume the air.

For those who desire privacy, secluded tables are available, complete with romantic lighting, and heaters for chilly weather.

For more than two decades, the Inn of the Seventh Ray has been serving gourmet California cuisine. The Inn makes use of organic ingredients whenever possible and accommodates special dietary needs.

Two longtime favorites are the Vegetarian Lasagna (layered with spinach and mushroom filling, ricotta cheese, pesto, and whole-wheat tomato noodles) and the North Atlantic Salmon (chargrilled and served with fennel champagne sauce).

The Inn prides itself on its luscious desserts, which are fruit juice sweetened. Don't miss the Tofu Cheesecake topped with blueberries. Another good choice is the Macadamia Nut Pie.

Angel Delight with Umeboshi Plum Sauce

Serves 4 as a main course

Owner Lucile Yaney describes Angel Delight with Umeboshi Plum Sauce as a "light but scrumptious choice at the Inn for vegetarians. We believe in giving you the purest of nature's foods, energized as a gift from the sun with a dash of esoteric food knowledge and ancient mystery school wisdom tossed in for seasoning and your pleasure."

3 tablespoons Asian sesame oil

1 pound seitan

1 cup bok choy, cut julienne

1 cup red and yellow bell pepper, cut julienne

1 cup shiitake mushrooms, cut julienne

1 medium portobello mushroom, thinly sliced

1/3 cup celery, cut julienne

1 teaspoon diced garlic

10 ounces udon noodles
Umeboshi Plum Sauce (recipe follows)
1 tablespoon sesame seeds

Umeboshi Plum Sauce
Makes about 1 cup
1 teaspoon sesame oil
2 large shallots, diced
1 teaspoon garlic, diced
$1^1/2$ cup organic white wine
3 tablespoons tamari
2 cups mushroom stock
$1^1/2$ tablespoons umeboshi vinegar
$1^1/2$ tablespoons umeboshi plum paste
Cornstarch to thicken

In a large pot of water, cook noodles until tender, about 10 minutes. Drain and keep warm.

In a large skillet over medium heat, heat oil and sauté seitan and vegetables until very crisp. Add garlic and plum sauce. Serve over noodles and sprinkle with sesame seeds.

In a medium pot, over medium heat, sauté oil, shallots, and garlic. Add wine and reduce by $1/2$. Add tamari, mushroom stock, vinegar, and plum paste. Bring to a boil. Thicken to a sauce-like consistency by adding cornstarch.

LONG LIFE VEGI HOUSE
2129 University Avenue
Berkeley, California 94704
510-845-6072

OPEN DAILY 11:30 A.M. TO 9:30 P.M.

Price: Inexpensive to moderate
Credit cards: AE, D, MC, V
Wheelchair accessible
No smoking
Alcohol: Wine and beer

This restaurant has long been famous locally for its vegetarian Chinese food. The menu lists more than forty vegetarian dishes. Owners David and Lily Tseng pride themselves on the fact that "absolutely no meat is used in any of the ingredients. It's a healthy place."

The Tsengs describe the restaurant as a "classical family-style Chinese restaurant," complete with Chinese paintings, Chinese lanterns, and lots of green — from plants to tablecloths to rugs. "It's all very casual, with a fresh feeling to it," David adds.

Start your meal off with an appetizer like Fresh Garlic Seaweed Salad or Pot Stickers. Among the most popular dishes are Vegi-Chicken (made with soy protein and black bean), Sauté Tofu with Vegetables, Vegi-Beef (made with wheat gluten), and Tofu with Spicy Hot Sauce.

Vegi-Chicken with String Beans in Black Bean Sauce

Serves 1 to 2 as a main course

"We selected the Vegi-Chicken recipe because it is simple to make at home," explains Lily Tseng. "It's a delicious meal that our customers keep asking for. It's delicious served with rice, hot from the pan."

$1/2$ teaspoon vegetable oil (optional)

1 teaspoon Chinese fermented black beans

1 tablespoon green onion, chopped

1 garlic clove

1 teaspoon minced fresh ginger

$1/2$ teaspoon red wine

1 tablespoon cornstarch mixed with 1 tablespoon water

$1/2$ teaspoon sugar

$1/2$ teaspoon ground pepper

1 to 2 tablespoons soy sauce

6 ounces soy protein ("vegi-chicken"), diced

4 ounces green beans

Steamed rice for serving

In a wok or large, heavy skillet over high heat, heat oil and stir-fry black beans for about 5 seconds. Add green onion, garlic, ginger, and stir-fry for 10 seconds. Add wine and cornstarch mixture, sugar, and pepper and stir-fry for 4 seconds. Add soy sauce, stir, and turn off heat. Stir until blended. Add "vegi-chicken" and green beans to sauce and stir to coat. Serve over hot rice.

NOTE: YOU CAN PAR-BOIL THE GREEN BEANS BEFORE ADDING TO SAUCE IF YOU WISH.

NATIVE FOODS

Smoke Tree Village
1775 East Palm Canyon Drive
Palm Springs, California 92264   *and*   73-890 El Paseo
Palm Desert, California 92260
760-416-0070   760-416-0070

www.palmsprings.com/health/nativefoods

OPEN MONDAY THROUGH SATURDAY 11 A.M. TO 9 P.M.

Price: Inexpensive to moderate
No credit cards
Wheelchair accessible
No smoking
No alcohol

This desert-community restaurant is great news for every vegetarian (and nonvegetarian!) looking for new and interesting dishes.

Located at the edge of a mall, behind the new post office, the Palm Springs eatery is the brainchild of chef and co-owner Tanya Petrovna, who previously ran successful vegetarian restaurants in Los Angeles and Orange County.

"What I always wanted to do was put together a restaurant that offered fresh, fun food — and this is it," states Tanya, who was described by a local newspaper as "the temptress of tofu."

Native Foods is small, but diners don't feel cramped because of the high ceilings. The ambiance is simple, with seven round tables featuring cactus centerpieces, lots of overhead fans, and decorative rugs on the wall. There is additional seating on an outside terrace. The restaurant has a clean, bright, and cheerful look. Food is served on paper plates, and the cups and utensils are plastic. Service is not only friendly and helpful, but enthusiastic as well.

Native Foods features three to four specials daily, plus a soup of the day. "Everything we serve is made from scratch with our own fresh tempeh and seitan," notes Tanya.

Among the popular dishes are the BBQ Love Sandwich (sliced seitan, caramelized onions, and barbecue sauce), hoagies, tacos, and yakisoba (Japanese buckwheat noodles stir-fried with cabbage, carrots, and onions).

At least three vegetarian burgers are offered on the menu, along with plenty of green salads and tasty side dishes such as Indonesian Tempeh Chips (sliced tempeh in a coconut milk batter, fried until crisp, and accompanied with an Indonesian soy sauce dip).

Very popular are the Jerk Steak Salad and Burger (homemade seitan marinated in Jamaican jerk spices), Tanya's Tiki Brochettes (grilled teriyaki-marinated chunks of textured vegetable protein), and the Chinese Salad (seitan, tossed greens, rice, tomato, corn, and sesame-orange dressing).

Treat yourself to a dessert — they're sugar- and dairy-free. Popular choices are the apple cobbler, carrot cake, and nondairy fudgesicles, but the Vegan Chocolate Cake is in the most demand.

Tijuana Tacos

Serves 6 to 8 as a main course

"These are recipes that reflect what I do," says Tanya, "which is try to prove that good-for-you food is not boring or bland — and what I cook, so you can understand and cook some too.

"Many of these dishes are 'native foods' — foods that are indigenous to a particular place and are healthy main staples. By using native foods for texture and combining them with flavors we are familiar with and love, great-tasting yet healthy foods become the reward."

1 cup textured vegetable protein (TVP), crumbled
3/4 cup water
1/4 cup olive or vegetable oil
1 onion, finely chopped
4 garlic cloves, minced
1 1/2 teaspoons sea salt
1 teaspoon ground coriander
1 teaspoon ground cumin
1/2 teaspoon red pepper flakes
6 to 8 corn tortillas
Shredded soy or nut cheese, salsa, shredded lettuce, and sliced avocado for serving

In a small saucepan, combine TVP and water. Bring to a boil, reduce heat, and simmer for 1 minute. Remove from heat, cover, and let sit for 5 to 10 minutes.

In a medium saucepan over medium-low heat, heat oil and sauté onion and garlic until lightly browned. Add TVP mixture, salt, cumin, and pepper flakes. Stir and cook for 1 minute. Remove from heat, cover, and let sit for 5 to 10 minutes.

Meanwhile, preheat oven to 350°F, wrap tortillas in aluminum foil, and heat in oven for 10 minutes.

Fill warm tacos with TVP mixture and top with one or more toppings.

Tofu Breakfast Scramble

Serves 2 to 4 as a breakfast side dish

1 tablespoon vegetable oil

$1/2$ cup finely chopped onion

$1/2$ red bell pepper, seeded, deribbed, and finely chopped

1 pound firm tofu, crumbled

$1/8$ teaspoon ground turmeric

$1/2$ teaspoon sea salt

$1/4$ teaspoon ground pepper

$1/2$ cup finely chopped green onions

In a medium skillet over medium heat, heat oil and sauté onion and bell pepper until tender. Add tofu, turmeric, salt, and pepper.

Sauté for 2 to 3 minutes, stirring until spices are well incorporated. Garnish with green onions and serve at once with breakfast potatoes, toast, and vegetarian sausage.

Killer Chocolate Cake

Makes one 8-inch cake

Tanya cautions that this cake is "not nonfat, but it is delicious and dairy-free."

1 cup unbleached all-purpose flour

$3/4$ cup unsweetened cocoa powder

2 teaspoons baking powder

1 cup canola oil

1 cup maple syrup

8 ounces tofu, drained for 20 minutes

2 teaspoons vanilla extract

1 cup chocolate chips (sweetened with barley malt)

Preheat oven to 375ºF. Lightly oil an 8-inch round cake pan.

Sift flour, cocoa powder, and baking powder into a medium bowl. In a blender, combine oil, syrup, tofu, and vanilla and puree until smooth.

Stir into flour mixture. Fold in chocolate chips. Pour into prepared pan and bake for 35 to 40 minutes, or until toothpick inserted in center comes out clean. Let cool completely on a wire rack before serving.

STRETCH'S CAFE
943 Orange Avenue
Coronado, California 92118
619-435-8886

OPEN MONDAY THROUGH SATURDAY 8 A.M. TO 9 P.M., SUNDAY TO 6 P.M.

Price: Inexpensive
Credit cards: None
Wheelchair accessible
No smoking
No alcohol

Stretch's is a charming, down-home, fun self-service cafe that has been owned and operated for 15 years by Stretch Maiden and his daughter Vicki.

The atmosphere is casual and the menu is filled with everything from hot and cold sandwiches and soups to healthy stuffed spuds and Mexican-style dishes. "The idea here is to provide healthy meals that taste great too," Stretch says. "Our menu is unique in that we're the only restaurant in town offering low-fat, and nonfat meals."

Located just four blocks south of the historic Hotel Del Coronado in the heart of town, locals opting for a healthy dining alternative soak up the homespun charm here and chow down on favorites like the Lite Lentil Burger, the Coronado Spud (a potato stuffed with steamed vegetables, chicken, and beans), or the popular house salads.

Another in-demand dish is the Chicken Quesadilla (sautéed mushrooms, olives, onions, chilies, tomatoes, chicken, and cilantro, served on a flour tortilla with melted jack cheese and topped with sour cream and avocado).

House favorites are indicated on the menu with a little chef symbol. Among them is a breakfast treat called the Philly Scramble (eggs with green chilies and Philadelphia cream cheese), and the Egg Burrito (three eggs scrambled with onions, olives, and chilies, rolled in a flour tortilla with beans and cheese, and served with avocado and sour cream on the side).

Spinach Fandango

Serves 2 as a main course

"The Spinach Fandango is awesome," says Vicki. "It's made of fresh or frozen spinach mixed with mushrooms, rice, jack cheese, and sour cream, and it's served casserole style. It's the most popular item on our menu and served with soup or salad and garlic bread."

One 10-ounce package frozen spinach, thawed and drained
1/2 cup cooked brown rice
1/2 cup sour cream
1 to 2 cups shredded Monterey jack cheese
4 to 6 fresh mushrooms, sliced
2 to 6 minced fresh basil leaves
2 to 4 tablespoons grated Parmesan cheese

Preheat oven to 350°F. Oil a casserole or baking dish.

In a medium bowl, combine spinach, rice, sour cream, jack cheese, and mushrooms. Mix well. Pour into prepared dish, spread evenly, and bake until bubbling hot, about 30 minutes. Garnish with basil and Parmesan and serve.

TILLIE GORT'S CAFE
111 Central Avenue
Pacific Grove, California 93950
408-373-0335

OPEN DAILY 11 A.M. TO 10:30 P.M.

Price: Moderate
Credit cards: AE, MC, V
Wheelchair accessible
No smoking
Alcohol: Beer and wine

Tillie Gort's restaurant and coffeehouse has been a fixture on the Monterey Bay penin-
sula for more than two decades. Located just three blocks from the aquarium and
Monterey's famous Cannery Row, the restaurant is a haven for tourists as well as locals.

Not much has changed here over the years. The barn-wood walls have been painted and
geraniums bloom in the window boxes out front. A mural covers the cafes ceiling, and local
artists display their paintings on the walls in a revolving exhibit.

Tillie's is a fifteen-table eatery (each one adorned with a homemade pinch pot filled
with flowers), and the outdoor seating area is the best people-watching spot in town.

The restaurant offers a wide variety of dishes, including No-Meat Loaf, a popular vegetarian favorite (a mixture of eggs, bread crumbs, yogurt, cheese, vegetables, almonds, herbs,

and spices, topped with marinara sauce and jack cheese).

Another popular choice is the All-in-One Plate (brown rice, black beans, and steamed vegetables with a choice of lemon-tahini sauce, tamari, or salsa. If you're in the mood for a great veggie burger, try the Mushroom Garden Burger (mushrooms, onions, oats, brown rice, cheese, and egg whites, topped with mushrooms and jack cheese on a whole-wheat bun).

Turkey burgers and regular burgers are also served here. For dessert, don't miss the homemade Black Bottom Cupcakes (chocolate cupcakes stuffed with cream cheese and chocolate chips). There's also a good selection of herbal teas, as well as espresso drinks, wine, and beer.

No-Meat Loaf

Serves 6 as a main course

"The No-Meat Loaf recipe is probably one of our oldest. It's been on our menu for 25 years. Other dishes have come and gone, but this one is always there. The cafe serves it topped with marinara sauce and melted cheese, and a choice of salad or baked potato."

2 loaves whole-wheat bread, diced

4 cups (1 pound) shredded Monterey jack cheese

3 onions, chopped

1 bunch celery, sliced thin

3 cups grated carrots

2 cups (8 ounces) slivered almonds

2 cups milk

2 cups chopped tomatoes

8 eggs, beaten

1 cup plain yogurt

1/4 cup minced garlic

1^1/2 tablespoons dried basil
1 tablespoon dried thyme
1 tablespoon dried oregano

Preheat oven to 350ºF. In a large bowl, combine all ingredients and mix until well blended. Form into a loaf shape, place in a baking pan, and bake for 1 hour, or until browned. Let cool completely before slicing and serving.

The Vegetarian Zone
2949 Fifth Avenue
San Diego, California 92103
619-298-7302

OPEN MONDAY THROUGH THURSDAY 11:30 A.M. TO 9 P.M., FRIDAY UNTIL 10 P.M., SATURDAY 8:30 A.M. TO 10 P.M., SUNDAY UNTIL 9 P.M.

Price: Moderate to expensive
Credit cards: D, MC, V
Wheelchair accessible
No smoking
Alcohol: Beer and wine

Located near Balboa Park, the Vegetarian Zone has been serving some of the best vegetarian cuisine in the San Diego area for more than two decades, and the praise it has received from food critics is evidence of that.

Natural Living Magazine described it as one of the top thirty vegetarian restaurants in the United States, while *Better Homes and Gardens* called the Vegetarian Zone "one of the top five most innovative vegetarian restaurants nationwide." For years, the restaurant has also been the favorite of the local media, one reviewer praising it as the best vegetarian restaurant in the San Diego area.

Thankfully, the restaurant hasn't let success spoil it. The decor remains tastefully simple. There are a few paintings on the walls and some hanging plants. The intimate dining room features booths and linen-covered tables with rattan chairs. By contrast, the outdoor dining patio is spectacular, with tree-sized potted plants, assorted colorful flowers, and a fountain.

The restaurant's philosophy is summed up on its menus: "Our intention is to serve you an international selection of vegetarian cuisine that is exciting to the taste, satisfying, and memorable."

Only quality ingredients are used, all free from chemical preservatives or dyes. No meat products, bleached white flour, or white or brown sugar is used in the preparation of any dish. Instead, honey, fruit juice, and maple syrup are used for sweeteners, and cheese is raw, rennetless, and undyed. Soy cheese and egg substitute may also be requested for most dishes.

For lunch or dinner, try the best-selling Spinach-Mushroom Lasagna (a variety of cheeses baked with spinach, fresh mushrooms, spinach pasta, and homemade marinara sauce, served with a vegetable medley).

Equally delicious is the Tofu Vegetable Enchilada (a spicy blend of tofu and vegetables inside a whole-wheat tortilla topped with Spanish sauce and guacamole) and the Layered Tofu Supreme (layers of tofu, spinach, pimientos, and mushrooms, topped with a gingered bell pepper sauce).

If you crave the taste of chicken, the Mock Chicken with Vegetables is perfect. As the menu notes, "it has more protein than the real thing and without the health and environmental liabilities."

On weekends, the Vegetarian Zone serves up a popular brunch. One favorite is the Southwest Tempeh Scramble (seasoned tempeh scrambled with hot and sweet peppers, red onions, and corn tortilla strips, topped with melted Cheddar and served with brown rice). Eggless and dairyless Scrambled Tofu and Tofu Ranchero (sautéed crumbled fresh tofu, black beans, red onions, chilies, corn, and cilantro) are both delicious.

The desserts are described on the menu as "enchanting," and that is no exaggeration. They are prepared in the restaurant's on-site bakery, with all-natural sweeteners. One of the most popular of these sweet treats is the Fruit Parfait Delight (whipped kefir cheese with fruit and maple syrup on a raisin-nut crust, topped with real whipped cream). The elegant and creamy rich Ricotta Cheesecake, high in protein yet low in calories, is also a favorite.

After dining, visit the combination gift shop and deli, which features a variety of foods and desserts to go, as well as an interesting selection of cookbooks, New Age music, and body-care products.

Maple Baked Custard

Serves 8 as a dessert

Owner Frank Russo says that Maple Baked Custard is his guests' favorite dessert. "It's a nutritious and delicious low-fat delight, the perfect light finale to a meal. Whether you're a longtime or a sometime vegetarian, you'll enjoy this dessert."

3 eggs

6 egg whites or $3/4$ cup Nulaid (95 percent egg-white product)

$1/3$ cup pure maple syrup

$2^1/2$ cups nonfat milk

3 heaping tablespoons protein powder (minimum of 7 grams protein per tablespoon)

$1/2$ teaspoon salt

$1/2$ teaspoon vanilla extract

$1/2$ teaspoon ground nutmeg

$1/2$ teaspoon ground cinnamon

1 cup sliced fresh, frozen, or canned (with water only) peaches

3 tablespoons slivered almonds

Preheat oven to 350ºF. In a blender, blend eggs and egg whites or Nulaid. With machine running, gradually add all remaining ingredients except peaches and almonds. Blend until smooth. Add half of peaches and blend until smooth. Pour into 8 custard cups.

Place cups in a deep baking pan and fill pan with hot water almost to the level of the custard. Bake for 20 minutes. Place remaining peaches on top of custard, then sprinkle with slivered almonds. Bake for 20 to 30 minutes, or until knife comes out clean. Remove cups from water bath and let cool at room temperature. Refrigerate to chill thoroughly before serving.

CITY SPIRIT CAFE
1343 Blake Street
Denver, Colorado 80202
303-575-0022

OPEN MONDAY THROUGH THURSDAY 11 A.M. TO 11 P.M., FRIDAY AND SATURDAY UNTIL 2 P.M.

Price: Moderate
All major credit cards
Wheelchair accessible
Smoking: In certain sections
Alcohol: Full service bar

When the City Spirit Cafe first opened its doors in 1986, it was among only a handful of restaurants in the then-rundown historic district on the fringe of Denver's downtown.

Today, the area known as LoDo (Lower Downtown) is the city's trendiest neighborhood, boasting more than eighty restaurants and art galleries. The cafe has changed along with the neighborhood.

What was originally conceived as a bookstore serving simple sandwiches like corned beef on rye is now better known for its nonalcoholic Smartinis, meatless lasagna, fabulous desserts, and cappuccino.

Although *trendy* might be an apt description of the City Spirit Cafe, it is also a comfortable, casual community hangout that provides a feast for the eyes as well as for the palate.

Housed in a historic building that used to be a sausage factory, the cafe, which seats seventy-five, features an ongoing art installation by artist-in-residence Susan Wick. Utilizing mosaic tiles and bright colors, Wick believes in changing the cafe's decor from time to time.

Even the small windows of the old factory are used as art; they are an ever-changing display that reflects the theme of whatever event is taking place in town that week or month. On weekends, the cafe is host to local bands that perform everything from rock 'n' roll to blues. The cafe is also a sponsor of special events through the year, such as a local fashion show and an ikebana (Japanese flower arranging) contest in July.

Everything here is made from scratch, with a minimal fat content. Whenever possible, organic ingredients are used in food preparation.

Appetizers include chips and salsa or spinach feta dip with cream cheese and jalapeno. The popular entrées are usually international in flavor, from a bowl of Japanese-style miso to the always-in-demand Middle Eastern Platter. The Healthy Burrito is a crowd pleaser (black beans and steamed vegetables wrapped in a red chili tortilla and topped with vegetarian green chili, Cheddar cheese, sour cream, and yogurt).

Another favorite is the Rice-Crust Pizza, with toppings ranging from pear, Gorgonzola, and walnuts to the more traditional tomato, basil, and cheese.

Baba Ghanouj

Serves 8 as an appetizer

"We care about your health," state City Spirit Cafe owners Mickey and Susan, "and these recipes reflect that attitude. The Baba Ghanouj and La Sal–Style Anasazi Beans are nutritious with qualities that make them ideal foods for the health-conscious person. They're also easy to prepare."

4 globe eggplants
1/2 cup tahini

4 garlic cloves
3 tablespoons fresh lemon juice
Salt and freshly ground pepper to taste
Pita bread for serving

Preheat oven to 425°F. Poke 15 to 20 holes in each eggplant, then place on a baking sheet and bake for 25 minutes, or until tender. Remove and let cool.

Remove skin from eggplants. In a blender or food processor, combine eggplant flesh, tahini, garlic, and lemon juice and puree until smooth. Add salt and pepper. Refrigerate in an airtight container for up to 3 days. Serve chilled, on pita bread.

Miso-Tahini Dressing

Makes 1 1/2 to 2 cups

"This dressing is a popular choice for the cafe's many salads. It's also great on sandwiches," says Mickey and Susan.

1/2 cup red barley miso
1/4 cup chopped onion
3/4 cup rice vinegar
1/2 cup tahini
1/2 teaspoon ground pepper
2 tablespoons sesame seeds
3/4 cup canola oil

In a blender or food processor, combine all ingredients except oil. Blend until smooth. With machine running, add oil slowly. Add water to desired consistency. Store in airtight container in refrigerator for up to 3 days.

La Sal–Style Anasazi Beans

Serves 4 as a side dish

"These delicious beans are served in the cafe's vegetarian burrito. They're also great served as a side dish."

2 cups (1 pound) dried Anasazi beans
1 strand kombu seaweed
1 tablespoon ground chipotle chili
1 red onion, finely chopped
3 Anaheim chilies, diced
3 garlic cloves
1 cup tomato sauce
2 tablespoons sea salt

Rinse and pick over beans. Soak overnight in water to cover by 2 inches. Drain. In a large pot, combine beans with water to cover by 2 inches. Add kombu, bring to a boil, reduce heat to a simmer, cover and cook until tender, about an hour. Add remaining ingredients and cook for 10 minutes.

CREATIVE CAFE
1837 Pearl Street
Boulder, Colorado 80302
303-449-1952

OPEN FOR LUNCH MONDAY THROUGH FRIDAY 11 A.M. TO 2 P.M.; DINNER SUNDAY THROUGH THURSDAY, 5 TO 9 P.M., FRIDAY AND SATURDAY UNTIL 9:30 P.M., BRUNCH SATURDAY AND SUNDAY 10 A.M. TO 3 P.M.

Price: Moderate
Credit cards: D, MC, V
Wheelchair accessible
No smoking
Alcohol: Organic wine and microbrews

Creative Cafe began as a Buddhist work-study project in 1989. Its current owners, Bobby and Sadhna Gupta, stumbled upon the cafe in 1995 and enjoyed the food and the atmosphere so much that they purchased it the same year.

Although they retained some of the most popular entrées from the old menu, such as Barbecued Tofu, and Spinach Lasagna, the Guptas made some additions. "The old menu had too much tofu and rice and basically nothing else," Bobby explains. "We don't need to eat so much protein, so we added more straight vegetarian dishes and balanced meals."

The cafe has won rave reviews over the years. It was named by the local daily as the best vegetarian restaurant in Boulder, and the *Vegetarian Journal* described it as the best vegetarian restaurant in Colorado.

Located on Pearl Street in Boulder's historic district, during the summer months the cafe's outdoor dining porch, with its overhead lattice-work and draping vines, offers a quiet respite from the street traffic. It's also a wonderful location for a glass of the restaurant's fine selection of organic wines.

Inside, a huge window runs the length of the front of the building and offers plenty of natural light for the many plants that adorn the Creative Cafe. Another attraction is the work of local artists which adorns the cafe's walls. On Sunday nights, live music is offered.

The menu reflects the seasons, changing in spring, summer, fall, and winter. All the cafe's food is organic, including the spices. The only canned product used is tomato sauce.

In addition to serving some of traditional favorites that reflect the owners' East Indian heritage, the menu borrows freely from other international cuisine. One of the most popular entrées is Dosa (an Indian rice and lentil crepe stuffed with potato-vegetable curry and served with a bowl of spicy samban). Another favorite is Nbeyaki Udon (a hearty miso soup brimming with udon noodles, tofu, bok choy, and other vegetables, served in an authentic cast-iron nab bowl).

A new addition to the menu is Portobello Mushroom Steaks (marinated in tamarind paste, grilled, topped with a reduction of red wine and onion, and served over basmati rice and vegetables). This is quickly becoming a best-seller.

Desserts include a guilt-free chocolate-tofu mousse, fresh fruit pie, and creamy tofu cheesecake topped with blueberries or cherries.

Earth and Sea Salad

Serves 4 to 6 as a side dish

Earth and Sea Salad sums up much of the Guptas philosophy about food. "This dish reflects the restaurant's Buddhist roots, and is a popular choice at the cafe." Sadhna adds that she hopes readers, when preparing this dish, will meditate about creating a planet where "we avoid killing or eating any living creature."

She continues: "I was raised Hindu, and in my mother's kitchen we would even abstain from eating leafy greens during the rainy season in order to avoid consuming any insects by mistake."

1 cup chopped baked tofu

1/4 cup peanut butter

1/4 cup tamari soy sauce

2 tablespoons olive oil

1 cup diced yellow squash

1 cup diced zucchini

1 cup broccoli florets

1 cup diced red bell pepper

1 cup diced carrots

1 cup diced red cabbage

1 cup arame seaweed soaked in water for 2 to 3 minutes and drained

2 tablespoons olive oil

1/4 cup balsamic vinegar

1/4 cup tamari soy sauce

To bake tofu: Preheat oven to 450°F. In a small bowl mix together peanut butter, tamari, and olive oil until smooth. Marinate tofu in mixture for 30 minutes. Bake for 30 minutes.

In a large bowl, combine all ingredients and mix well.

BLOODROOT
85 Ferris Street
Bridgeport, Connecticut 06605
203-576-9168

OPEN FOR LUNCH TUESDAY AND THURSDAY THROUGH SATURDAY, 11:30 A.M. TO 2:30 P.M.; BRUNCH SUNDAY
11:30 A.M. TO 2:30 P.M.; DINNER TUESDAY AND THURSDAY 6 TO 9 P.M., FRIDAY AND SATURDAY UNTIL 10 P.M.

Price: Moderate to expensive
No credit cards; personal checks accepted
Wheelchair accessible
No smoking
Alcohol: Beer and wine

This very popular feminist-run restaurant and bookstore has been serving up exquisite vegetarian cuisine for more than two decades. Located on an inlet of Long Island Sound at the end of a small dead-end street, the restaurant's excellent view of the sound makes it the perfect site for alfresco dining.

The outdoor terrace is surrounded by herb and flower gardens, and behind the restaurant guests will discover another feast for the eyes: organic vegetable gardens.

The quiet, peaceful indoor dining area is furnished with tables and chairs from different eras, which adds to the room's old-fashioned charm. Enhancing this bygone-era atmosphere is a long wall covered with hundreds of photographs of women.

Diners select their meals and beverages from a blackboard menu. The restaurant offers a seasonal vegetarian menu, and entries change every three weeks. Vegan dishes are available and indicated on the blackboard by asterisks. Ingredients and methods of preparation are available on request.

Almost all the vegetables served here are organically grown, many from the restaurant's own garden.

After paying for their meal, guests bring the receipt to the kitchen counter where their food is prepared. In this self-service arrangement, guests are called by name when their food is ready, and they also clear their own tables. "This system produces an informal atmosphere and a feeling of parity between workers and visitors," the collective maintains.

Among the popular dishes served here are Oatmeal Sunflower Bread, Marinated Tofu and Chinese Cabbage Salad, and Brown Rice Pudding.

Also located on the premises is Sanguinaria Publishing, an independent feminist publishing venture that is also operated by the collective. This press offers an interesting variety of cookbooks, such as *The Perennial Political Palate.*

Tempeh-Stuffed Baked Potatoes

Serves 6 as a main course

Selma Miriam, of the Bloodroot Collective says, "We chose the Tempeh-Stuffed Baked Potatoes recipe because it appeals to vegetarians and nonvegetarians alike. It is not very difficult or time-consuming to make, and the potatoes store readily in the refrigerator for a week or so. It's hearty, savory food, and it's a good leftover too."

6 large Idaho potatoes, scrubbed
1/2 cup soy milk
1 1/2 teaspoons salt

Freshly ground pepper to taste

2 tablespoons olive oil

One 8-ounce cake tempeh, diced

$1^1/2$ onions, chopped

1 large celery stalk, including leaves, chopped

8 ounces white mushrooms, sliced

$3/4$ teaspoon ground coriander

1 garlic clove, crushed

3 tablespoons dry sherry

$1^1/2$ tablespoons fresh lemon juice

$1/2$ cup minced fresh parsley

Paprika for sprinkling

Bake potatoes in a 400ºF oven for 1 hour, or until tender. Slice off $1/2$-inch of skin on top and scoop out potato flesh. Using an electric mixer, mash potato flesh until fluffy. Beat in soy milk and salt and pepper to taste. Set aside.

In a large skillet over medium heat, heat olive oil and sauté tempeh until well browned. Add onion, celery, and mushrooms and sauté until well browned. Add coriander, salt, and garlic and sauté until very well browned. Turn off heat and stir in sherry, lemon juice, and parsley.

Add vegetable mixture to potatoes and stir to blend. Taste and correct seasoning. Restuff potato skins, piling mixture high. Sprinkle with paprika. Refrigerate until serving time.

When ready to serve, heat potatoes 20 to 30 minutes in a preheated 400ºF oven. Steamed broccoli and carrots may be served alongside, and miso gravy is nice, though not necessary, to serve over potatoes.

Recipe comes from *The Second Seasonal Political Palate* by the Bloodroot Collective, Sanguinaria Publishing, Bridgeport, CT 06605.

NATURE'S FOOD PATCH DELI/CAFE
1225 Cleveland Street
Clearwater, Florida 33755
813-443-6703

OPEN MONDAY THROUGH SATURDAY 11 A.M. TO 3 P.M.; DELI OPEN MONDAY THROUGH SATURDAY 9 A.M. TO 9 P.M., SUNDAY 10 A.M. TO 7 P.M.

Price: Inexpensive to moderate
Credit cards: MC, V
Wheelchair accessible
No smoking
Alcohol: Sold but not served

Tucked in the back of a natural foods store is a cafe that is one of Clearwater's best-kept secrets.

The interior projects a mood of earthy warmth, highlighted by wood furnishings, plants, and paintings by local artists. The mood is enhanced by strains of light jazz and classical music playing softly in the background.

The cafe menu features a variety of stir-fried vegetable dishes, as well as favorites like Red-Chili Tortilla Quesadilla and their Walnut Veggie Burger.

Daily specials are served, along with two hot soups. As a perfect end to a healthy lunch, sample one of the cafe's many organic desserts, such as traditional Carrot Cake (dairy or nondairy), Tofu-Chocolate Dream Pie, Coconut Dream Pie, sugar- and dairy-free Banana Nut Muffins, and the always-popular Tofu Peanut Butter Pie.

The cafe is attached to a gourmet deli that boasts over fifty healthful offerings, many of which are completely organic. The list includes free-range Turkey Meat Loaf, Blackened or Barbecued Tofu, Satay Udon Pasta Salad, and eggless Tofu Egg Salad.

The deli also makes hearty sandwiches on whole-grain breads, with a choice of traditional or eggless potato salad. Many are pre-packaged for people in a hurry who want something light.

Tropical Thai Curry

Serves 4 as a main course

"The Tropical Thai Curry is a daily special our chef whips up that will knock your socks off," asserts food service director Ted Tillson. "It's one of the most requested meals at our cafe. This dish should be served with basmati rice."

SAUCE
4 tablespoons oil
1/2 cup finely chopped green bell pepper
1/2 cup finely chopped onion
4 tablespoons smooth natural peanut butter
2 bananas, mashed
2 cups light coconut milk
2 tablespoons chopped fresh basil
2 tablespoons curry powder
2 teaspoons turmeric

1 teaspoon salt
4 tablespoons honey

VEGETABLES
4 tablespoons oil
$1/2$ cup finely chopped onion
1 cup cooked chickpeas
1 cup finely diced zucchini
1 cup finely diced broccoli
1 cup finely diced cauliflower
1 cup finely diced carrots
6 ounces white mushrooms, sliced
2 cups finely diced tofu

To make sauce: In a large, heavy saucepan over medium heat, heat oil and sauté pepper and onion. Add peanut butter and banana, reduce heat to low, and blend. Add all remaining ingredients. Stir together, bring to a light simmer (do not boil), and remove from heat. Set aside and keep warm.

In a wok or large skillet over medium-high heat, heat oil and stir-fry vegetables and tofu for 2 to 3 minutes. Add sauce. Cover and cook for 2 minutes, or until vegetables are crisp-tender. Spoon over rice and serve.

UNICORN PLACE FINE VEGETARIAN CUISINE
220 Sandy Springs Circle
Atlanta, Georgia 30328
404-252-1165

OPEN MONDAY THROUGH SATURDAY 11 A.M. TO 9 P.M., SUNDAY 5 TO 9 P.M.

Price: Moderate
Credit cards: AE, D, DC, MC, V
Wheelchair accessible
No smoking
No alcohol

Diners who visit this totally vegan Georgia restaurant will find an elegantly casual and cozy atmosphere and an incredible collection of unicorn figurines from around the world. Even the drawings and paintings on the walls depict unicorns.

This thirteen-table eatery located in Atlanta's business district attracts mostly local businessmen and vegetarians from throughout the city who appreciate the restaurant's sugar-free, low-fat, and low-salt meals.

The booths here are comfortable, the atmosphere is relaxing, and the attention to the food is so meticulous that filtered water is used to make the ice cubes.

Two of the most popular menu items are the Italian Veggie Meatballs, and the Veggie Burger. The Southern-Fried Tofu is always in demand. Excellent salads are prepared here using only organically raised produce.

Daily specials are featured, along with sandwiches and an excellent pasta of the day. For dessert, try the sensational carrot cake. To quench your thirst, order something from the juice bar, with its many nourishing offerings.

Southern-Fried Tofu

Serves 2 as a main course

"Southern-Fried Tofu is truly finger-lickin' good," states the restaurant. "Straight from Georgia, it can be served with anything from beans to fried green tomatoes.

"Don't let the ingredients fool you — this is actually simple to prepare and features a perfect combination of seasonings. This is an excellent entrée, served with rice and vegetables, or the makings for a delicious sandwich filling with eggless mayonnaise, lettuce, and tomato."

$1/2$ pound firm low-fat tofu, rinsed and cut into $1/2$-inch-thick slices

$2/3$ cup low-fat rice milk or soy milk

2 teaspoons fresh lemon juice

$1^1/2$ cups nutritional yeast

2 teaspoons salt

1 teaspoon garlic powder

1 teaspoon onion powder

1 teaspoon dried parsley

$1/2$ teaspoon paprika

$1/2$ teaspoon dried tarragon

$1/2$ teaspoon dried dillweed

$1/2$ teaspoon dried basil

$1/2$ teaspoon dried oregano

$1/2$ teaspoon curry powder

$1/4$ teaspoon dry mustard

$1/4$ teaspoon dried rosemary

$1/4$ teaspoon celery seed

$2/3$ cup whole-wheat pastry flour

1 tablespoon canola oil

Drain tofu on paper towels and pat dry. In a shallow bowl, mix milk and lemon juice. In another shallow bowl, mix yeast, salt, herbs, and spices.

Dredge each tofu piece in flour, then dip into milk mixture. Dredge in seasoning mix, coating entire piece.

In a large skillet over medium-high heat, heat oil and cook tofu until browned on both sides.

EARTH
738 North Wells Street
Chicago, Illinois 60610
312-335-5475

OPEN FOR LUNCH MONDAY THROUGH SATURDAY 11:30 A.M. TO 2:30 P.M.; DINNER 5:30 TO 9 P.M.

Price: Moderate to expensive
All major credit cards
Wheelchair accessible
No smoking
Alcohol: Wine

Located in Chicago's hip River North neighborhood, Earth is a healthy respite from the local club scene. Owner Barry Bursak is a man with a mission: "to serve delicious food made with predominantly organic and environmentally friendly ingredients." Even the restaurant's beautiful hickory floor came from an environmental project created to save wood that was intended to be turned into sawdust.

There is an austere and almost Zen-like quality to the decor. The restaurant's stark white walls are ornamented only by small shelves displaying unusually shaped clear glass vases with dried flower arrangements. In the center of the dining room is a huge fiddle-leaf fig tree.

A popular dinner appetizer is small sweet mussels steamed in herbed apple cider. Most of the other starters are lavish salads, such as Roasted Beets and Red Onions in balsamic soy dressing, or Blue Caesar with Amish blue cheese.

One favorite lunch selection is the Roasted Vegetable Sandwich (fresh goat cheese and roasted vegetables on seven-grain bread). A popular dinner dish is the Vegetable Strudel, served with or without shrimp (filo dough layered with shredded vegetables, flavored with sesame and soy). Another favorite entrée is the Grilled Mahimahi, with mashed potatoes and ginger-mustard sauce.

The desserts are delicious. Recommended is Angel Food Cake, served with a fresh fruit compote. Beverages include vegetable juices and organic wines.

Earth Vegetable-Tomato Stew with Cardamom

Serves 2 to 4 as a main course

Barry Bursak selected this stew because "it is a popular choice on the dinner menu, and also because it is representative of what we do — balanced with lots of different tastes and textures." This recipe was adapted for home kitchens by chef Charles Warshawsky.

1 yellow onion

1 red onion

4 carrots

2 celery stalks

1 leek

1 yellow zucchini

1 green zucchini

4 large boiling potatoes

1 tablespoon canola oil

1 each red, green, and yellow bell pepper, seeded, deribbed, and coarsely chopped

4 garlic cloves, minced

1 tablespoon ground cardamom

28 ounces canned diced tomatoes

$1/3$ cup tomato paste

2 bay leaves

$1/4$ cup minced fresh thyme

$1/4$ teaspoon dried oregano

1 cup cooked lentils

$1/2$ cup cooked kidney beans

$1/2$ cup cooked chickpeas

Salt and ground pepper, to taste

Juice of 1 lemon

Steamed brown rice for serving

Cut onions, carrots, celery, leek, zucchini, and potatoes into 1/2-inch dice. In a soup pot over low heat, heat oil and sauté diced vegetables and peppers until soft, not brown. Add garlic and half of cardamom and cook for 5 minutes. Add tomatoes, tomato paste, and herbs and cook for 15 minutes. Add beans and cook for 15 minutes, or until potatoes are tender.

Taste and season with remaining cardamom, salt, pepper, and lemon juice. Serve with brown rice.

PATTIE'S QUICK & LIGHT
700 North Michigan Avenue
Chicago, Illinois, 60614
312-751-7777

OPEN MONDAY THROUGH FRIDAY 9 A.M. TO 7 P.M., SATURDAY 10 A.M. TO 6 P.M.; SUNDAY NOON TO 5 P.M.

Price: Inexpensive
No credit cards
Wheelchair accessible
No smoking
No alcohol

Pattie's Quick & Light is a downtown oasis for health-conscious, calorie-counting, cholesterol-wary, and clock-watching office workers, company executives, and tourists on Chicago's Michigan Avenue.

Located on the city's Magnificent Mile in the eighth-floor food court of Chicago Place Mall, it is an ideal breakfast, lunch, or dinner stop for the shop-till-you-drop crowd that scours this busy, upscale shopping district.

It all began seven years ago when owner Pattie Ruppert — then working a sales job in a downtown office building — noticed that the busiest lunch spots were the salad bars, not the fast-food courts.

Less than a year later, she opened Pattie's, and in 1995 won a *Chicago Magazine* commendation as one of the top healthy restaurants in the Windy City.

The decor is custom imprinted Italian tiles and maple counters. There is a stand-up counter along one wall and seating for 200 in the beautiful food court atrium, complete with skylights, lush trees, and fountains.

Any similarity between Pattie's and the other fast food eateries in the mall ends right there, because this restaurant's menu strictly adheres to the American Heart Association's guidelines for a Healthy Heart Diet: No dogs, greasy fries, or chocolate shakes served here.

For breakfast, there is a Hearty Sandwich (a whole-wheat English muffin, turkey Canadian bacon, egg whites, and low-fat American cheese) only 4 grams of fat and 350 calories. Other breakfast options are Whole-Wheat French Toast and low-fat muffins.

Lunchtime features daily soups and specials in addition to the regular menu. A popular house specialty is Jamaican Jerk Chicken, with red beans and rice. For vegetarians, a good choice is Homemade Vegetarian Chili, and various vegetarian pizzas.

The restaurant also offers veggie and buffalo burgers, pizzas, salads, and sandwiches. An Italian sandwich favorite is Vegetarian Focaccia (grilled onions, eggplant, red peppers, tomato, artichokes, zucchini, and low-fat mozzarella baked in focaccia bread).

Beverages include fresh-squeezed juices, bottled water, and herbal teas, fruit smoothies, and nonfat yogurt shakes.

Pesto Sauce

Makes about 4 cups

Owner Pattie Ruppert points out that traditional pesto is very high fat, unlike this low-fat version.

"This pesto has a wide variety of uses. Try it tossed with penne pasta, strips of grilled chicken, chopped fresh basil, and golden raisins, topped with chopped tomatoes and a touch of Parmesan and black pepper. It's also excellent on hot or cold sandwiches."

2 cups fat-free mayo
$1/4$ cup chopped garlic
2 cups water
$1/2$ cup thawed frozen chopped spinach
1 cup (8 ounces) grated Parmesan cheese
1 cup packed fresh basil leaves

In a blender, combine all ingredients, in batches if necessary, and blend until smooth. Store in an airtight container in refrigerator for up to 3 days.

GREATEST GRAINS
1600 Harrison Street
Davenport, Iowa 52803
319-323-7521

OPEN MONDAY THROUGH FRIDAY 9 A.M. TO 8 P.M., SATURDAY TO 6 P.M., SUNDAY NOON TO 5 P.M.

Price: Inexpensive
Credit cards: MC, V; checks accepted for exact amount
Wheelchair accessible
No smoking
No alcohol; nonalcoholic wine available

Greatest Grains natural foods deli and market has been a family-run operation since 1979. Three generations participate in different facets of the business.

The deli is housed in a vintage 1900 building on the fringe of downtown Davenport. The store was originally used as a butcher shop and an A&P grocery store, before being converted into a restaurant and market.

There are about eight tables which can seat thirty people, and patrons range from shoppers to local businesspeople. "Everyone in town eats here," proclaims marketing director Candice Campbell. "With the original hardwood floors in the dining area, there's a wonderful old-corner-store feeling here — there's a ma-and-pa flavor to it."

Besides the deli, the store has a successful market, bakery, bulk food, and catering service. The knowledgeable staff can answer queries on the homeopathic remedies and vitamin supplements sold here.

The prepared foods include a wide variety of dishes, and everything is made from scratch daily, from organic ingredients (when in season).

Down-home deli favorites include vegetarian and nonvegetarian dishes, salads, gourmet soups, and sandwiches. Other popular dishes include Tabbouleh Salad, Kashi, and Hummus. Desserts include Fruit Crisps, brownies, and cookies baked fresh daily.

Traditional Pasta Salad

Serves 10 as a side dish

"We selected the Traditional Pasta Salad recipe because of its classic taste, says Campbell. "The blend of fresh herbs, olive oil, spices, tomatoes, and warm pasta is invigorating not only to the nose, but the palate as well.

"This is one of our favorite and most requested meals. It is the kind of thing you get cravings for. Once you try it, you just can't get enough. We call this a 'play with it' recipe because there are no set amounts. Keep adding and tasting until the amounts are to your taste.

"This recipe is easy to make at home with basic and inexpensive ingredients. It is low in fat and calories but contains many of the essential nutrients that go into a well-balanced meal.

"The recipe fits in with our 'made from scratch' motif, and it is not time-consuming to make. The ingredients can be adjusted to fit a family of four or a catered party of hundreds."

SAUCE
1 cup olive oil
1/2 cup grated mozzarella cheese
1/4 cup fresh basil, finely chopped
1/4 cup fresh lemon juice

2 garlic cloves, minced

$1/4$ cup red wine vinegar

Ground pepper to taste

4 fresh tomatoes, peeled, seeded, and diced

4 cups fusilli or shell pasta (cooked)

$1/4$ cup grated Parmesan

To make sauce: In a large bowl, combine oil, mozzarella, basil, lemon juice, garlic, vinegar, and pepper. Stir in tomatoes.

In a large pot of salted boiling water, cook pasta until al dente, about 10 minutes. Drain, rinse, and drain again. Add to sauce. (If pasta is warm, cheese will melt. Our customers like it best this way.) Sprinkle with Parmesan and more pepper to taste. Serve at once, or let cool and serve at room temperature.

SISTERS CAFE
5313 West 94th Terrace
Prairie Village, Kansas 66217
913-381-9615

Price: Inexpensive
No credit cards
Wheelchair accessible
No smoking
No alcohol

Sisters Cafe is a dream come true for twin sisters Colleen and Christine Bover, whose family tree has several restaurateurs in its branches.

"Our father and grandparents cooked with all the love they had, and we want to carry forward that way of serving food that nurtures the body and spirit," Christine says.

The small cafe, which is located next to a health food store, very much reflects that philosophy. It exudes a comfortable, homey atmosphere, and Colleen and Christine do all they can to reinforce that ambiance by giving their guests lots of personal attention.

You'll be invited to browse the cafe's bookshelves while waiting for your lunch. Should you wish to linger over your herbal tea while catching up with an old friend, no one is going to scoot you out. "We want you to make the cafe your home away from home," asserts Colleen.

The cafe offers an interesting selection of soups, salads, sandwiches, and juices. One of the most popular lunch options is the Veggie Stir-Fry (organic vegetables tossed with fresh ginger, garlic, sesame oil, and tamari soy sauce, then lightly steamed and served over a bed of rice).

A unique grilled sandwich is the Veggie Aioli (roasted peppers, zucchini, onions, potatoes, mushroom, carrots, garlic, and other seasonal vegetables heaped on multi-grain bread with a basil-mayo spread and choice of cheese. The sandwich is then dry grilled).

Tofu-Spinach Quiche

Makes one 9-inch pie; serves 6

"The Tofu-Spinach Quiche is requested every day by our customers. Maybe it's because this low-fat delight tastes like it's loaded with cheese, but actually there's none at all. Whatever the reason, this is one of our all-time favorite main courses. It will please all who try it."

WHOLE-WHEAT PASTRY CRUST

$1^1/2$ cups whole-wheat pastry flour

$1/2$ teaspoon fine sea salt

$1/2$ cup plus 1 tablespoon canola oil

3 tablespoons plus $1^1/2$ teaspoons ice water

FILLING

1 pound firm tofu, crumbled

$1/4$ cup brown rice vinegar

1 teaspoon onion powder

1 teaspoon fine sea salt

$1/2$ teaspoon dry mustard

1 tablespoon olive oil

1 onion, finely chopped

1 garlic clove, minced

6 ounces white mushrooms, thinly sliced

1 tablespoon tamari soy sauce

1 pound fresh spinach, well washed, stemmed, and chopped

1/4 cup tightly packed fresh basil leaves, finely chopped

1 large tomato, sliced

To make crust: Preheat oven to 350°F. In a medium bowl, stir flour and salt together. Add oil and water and stir until it forms a crumbly meal. Gather into a ball (dough will be moist). Press evenly and firmly into bottom and up sides of a 9-inch pie plate to make a 1/2-inch ridge above edge of plate. Bake until light golden, 20 to 25 minutes. Let cool.

To make filling: In a blender, combine tofu, vinegar, onion powder, salt, and mustard and blend until smooth. Transfer to a large bowl. In a large skillet over medium heat, heat oil and sauté onion, garlic, mushrooms, and tamari until mushrooms are browned, about 6 minutes.

Add spinach, cover, and cook until spinach is wilted, about 2 to 3 minutes. Uncover and cook, stirring constantly, until moisture is gone, about 3 minutes. Add mixture to tofu along with basil and stir to mix.

Pour into baked crust. Arrange tomato slices overlapping in a circle on top. Bake until lightly browned and firm in center, 40 to 50 minutes. Let cool for 15 minutes. Serve warm.

ALFALFA
557 South Limestone
Lexington, Kentucky 40508
606-253-0014

OPEN FOR LUNCH MONDAY THROUGH FRIDAY 11 A.M. TO 2 P.M.; BRUNCH SATURDAY AND SUNDAY 10 A.M. TO 2 P.M.; DINNER TUESDAY THROUGH THURSDAY 5:30 TO 9 P.M., FRIDAY AND SATURDAY UNTIL 10 P.M.

Price: Inexpensive to Moderate
Credit cards: MC, V
No wheelchair access
No smoking
Alcohol: Wine and beer

This small natural foods restaurant seats sixty-four people and is housed in an old building across the street from the campus of the University of Kentucky and not far from Lexington's downtown business district. The clientele is largely made up of faculty and local businesspeople enjoying Alfalfa's creative vegetarian delights.

The casual, cheerful atmosphere here immediately makes guests feel right at home. The windowsills are lined with plants, and the floors are covered with well-trod carpets. Some of the Formica tables date back 27 years to when the cafe had to barter food for furnishings.

Artwork by local artists decorate the walls. In the rear can be found a small stage where most evenings musicians provide world music to add a spicy flavor to the place.

The food served at Alfalfa's emphasizes regional as well as international specialties, such as Hoppin' John (rice topped with black-eyed peas in tomato sauce, topped with green peppers, onions, and Cheddar cheese), and Red Beans with Rice, topped with Cheddar cheese. Also a favorite are the house-made breads and pastries.

The menu offers a variety of interesting vegetarian entrées, as well as a nice assortment of salads made with organic greens whenever possible. During the summer months, Alfalfa buys most of its produce from local farmers.

Desserts are a specialty of the house. Highly recommended are the cheesecake, apple, or cherry pies, and the delicious house-made whole-wheat and chocolate chip cookies. If you're thirsty, try one of the natural colas.

Hoppin' John

Serves 4 to 6 as a main course

Hoppin' John is the cafe's signature dish. Chef Jess writes: "It's a traditional Southern dish that's usually served on New Year's for good luck. Every time I make it I think about my favorite Carson McCullers novel. In it, she writes about 'walking a mile for some Hoppin' John.'"

TOMATO SAUCE

8 cups diced tomatoes

1 cup dry red wine

6 tablespoons chopped basil

1 tablespoon butter or olive oil

2 teaspoons ground pepper

2 tablespoons minced fresh parsley

2 bay leaves

1 tablespoon salt

1 tablespoon honey or molasses
6 ounces tomato paste

2 cups canned black-eyed peas
Steamed rice for serving
Shredded white Cheddar cheese, finely diced onions, and finely diced green bell
    pepper for garnish

To make sauce: In a large saucepan, combine all ingredients except tomato paste and stir well. Bring to a boil, reduce heat, cover, and simmer for 1 hour. Stir in tomato paste until well blended. Warm black-eyed peas. Serve black-eyed peas over steamed rice. Top with some tomato sauce. Sprinkle with cheese, onions, and bell peppers.

EARTHEREAL RESTAURANT AND BAKERY
3309 Line Avenue
Shreveport, Louisiana 71104
318-865-8497

OPEN MONDAY THROUGH FRIDAY 9:30 A.M. TO 4:30 P.M.

Price: Inexpensive
No credit cards
Wheelchair accessible
No smoking
No alcohol

Owner Katie Koellen says that when she and her husband, John, decided in 1986 to expand their storefront natural foods restaurant to its present size, they wanted an open-kitchen design. What was once simply a vitamin store and a "hippie health food" cafe thus became a full restaurant with fifteen tables and its own on-site bakery. Gone was the simple salad and sandwich menu, replaced by one that featured everything from elaborate salads to muffins, breads, and blended fruit drinks.

This new concept suited John just fine. A chef from a family of restaurateurs, he was used to working in large-scale posh restaurants and resorts from Phoenix to upstate New York.

The atmosphere at Earthereal is far from posh, though — down-home is more like it. Don't expect to find linen and lace on the tables. Instead, you will find fresh flowers on each table and a cozy, friendly atmosphere.

Earthereal Restaurant and Bakery is located in a 1920s brick building in an older residential section of Shreveport, at the end of what used to be the trolley line that abutted the Delta cotton fields.

Although this is Dixie, the menu is more reflective of trendy California than the South. And it isn't that Southern favorite, iced tea, that's in demand here, but smoothies (fruit juices, banana, honey, and ice blended with a choice of fruit).

Favorites on the menu range from Soymeat or Avocado Tacos to sandwiches such as the Avocado Special (avocado, mushrooms, carrots, cheese, onions, tomatoes, and sprouts), and the Scott Special (soymeat, tabbouleh, soy bits, cheese, mustard, olives, and sprouts). Another popular sandwich is the Christopher (avocado, mushrooms, soy bits, tabbouleh, olives, onions, pickles, tomatoes, sunflower seeds, and sprouts).

Salads are also in demand. There's the Harmony (lettuce, zucchini, cheese, mushrooms, carrots, tomatoes, mushrooms, cucumbers, sprouts, sunflower seeds, soy bits, and dressing), and the Avocado au Gratin (avocado with choice of cottage cheese, egg salad, chicken, or tuna salad on lettuce with olives, sprouts, and vegetables, with fresh-fruit dressing on the side). Many of the herbs used in these salads are grown in the garden behind the restaurant.

A daily vegetarian special is offered — anything from eggplant lasagna to mushroom enchiladas. The fragrant and tasty breads, muffins, and cookies — all fresh from the oven — will remind you of Saturday afternoon at Grandma's house.

The Koellens like to improvise and adapt recipes — but the goal is always the same: "Cut the oil, omit the salt, and reduce the sugar."

Earthereal Vegetable Soup

Serves 6 to 8 as an appetizer

"The Earthereal Vegetable Soup has always been a popular favorite at the restaurant," Katie states. "It's very hearty and healthy, and also the perfect choice for those on a diet. It's a good combination with sandwiches and salads."

4 quarts water

$1^1/2$ cups chopped tomatoes

$2/3$ cup tomato paste

1 onion, chopped

1 cup chopped carrots

1 cup chopped celery

1 cup chopped potatoes

1 cup chopped cucumber

1 cup chopped zucchini

1 cup chopped cabbage

1 cup chopped broccoli

1 cup chopped cauliflower

1 cup chopped mushrooms

1 cup corn

1 bell pepper, seeded, deribbed, and chopped

2 bay leaves

2 teaspoons dried sweet basil

$1/2$ teaspoon salt

In a large soup pot, combine all ingredients and bring to a boil. Reduce heat, cover, and simmer until vegetables are tender, about 30 minutes.

THE ORCHARD RESTAURANT
45 North Market Street
Frederick, Maryland 21701
301-663-4912

OPEN TUESDAY THROUGH SATURDAY 11:30 A.M. TO 2:30 P.M. AND 5 TO 9 P.M.

Price: Moderate
Credit cards: AE, D, DC, MC, V
Wheelchair accessible
No smoking
Alcohol: Beer and wine

"People who enter the restaurant all say: 'I love the colors!'" states co-owner Jim Hickey, and there is, indeed, a colorful flavor to this restaurant, which offers the ambiance of a sophisticated bistro.

The walls are covered with modern handmade quilts, African mud cloth, and artwork from some of Frederick's best artists. Large windows are draped with beautiful and colorful tapestry curtains and splash the restaurant — and artwork — with lots of light. The restaurant's floors are made of hardwood offset with quarry tile.

For diners who enjoy soothing sounds with their meals, live music is offered on Saturday evenings and features classical guitar, lute, and harp.

The Orchard Restaurant specializes in stir-fries and tempura. Homemade soups, dressings, sauces, breads, and desserts are also trademarks of this natural foods eatery. All the food prepared here is homemade and only natural ingredients are used. Organically grown products are utilized when available.

For customers seeking a bit more than vegetables, some chicken and seafood dishes are on the menu.

Indonesian Stir-Fry

Serves 6 as a main course

Owners Jim and Eileen Hickey chose the Indonesian Stir-Fry because "it is probably our most popular dish." Jim adds: "The sauce can be used in many ways. It can be reduced and tossed with noodles and topped with grilled chicken, or poured into a plate swirled with pureed cilantro and topped with grilled calamari for an appetizer. The reduced sauce can also be used to marinate skewers of ingredients for grilled authentic Indonesian satays."

PEANUT LIME SAUCE
3/4 cup tamari soy sauce
1/4 cup honey
1/2 cup smooth natural peanut butter
1/2 cup dry white wine
1/2 cup fresh lime juice
1 1/2 teaspoons minced garlic
1 1/2 teaspoons minced fresh ginger
1 teaspoon cayenne pepper
1 3/4 cups water
2 to 4 tablespoons Asian sesame oil
1 to 1 1/2 pounds cubed tofu or chicken, or medium shrimp, peeled and deveined

10 cups julienned vegetables, such as bell peppers, onions, carrots, mushrooms,
    bok choy
Steamed brown rice or cooked soba noodles for serving

To make sauce: combine first 6 ingredients in a medium bowl and whisk until blended.

In a large wok or skillet over medium-high heat, heat oil and stir-fry tofu, chicken, or
shrimp for 2 minutes. Add vegetables and sauce and cook until sauce is reduced and thickened and vegetables are crisp-tender, 2 to 3 minutes. Serve over brown rice or toss with soba
noodles.

THYME SQUARE
4735 Bethesda Avenue
Bethesda, Maryland 20814
301-657-9077

OPEN SUNDAY THROUGH THURSDAY, 11 A.M. TO 10 P.M., FRIDAY AND SATURDAY TO 11 P.M.

Price: Moderate to expensive
Credit cards: AE, MC, V
Wheelchair accessible
No smoking
Alcohol: Organic wines

One of the newest natural foods restaurants in the metropolitan D.C. area, this Bethesda hot spot is the creation of Mark Caraluzzi, and his wife, Tracy, who operate a number of successful local restaurants, including the award-winning Bistro Bistro.

Thyme Square, which opened in 1996, is an upscale gourmet dining experience. This eatery uses mostly organically grown foods and promotes a partnership with local cooperatives and farmers in order to obtain the freshest ingredients.

At Thyme Square, vegetables inspire the cooking as well as the decor. Baskets of produce are located everywhere throughout the restaurant, and the dining room resembles a tropical garden.

Designed by award-winning restaurant designer Olvea Demetriou, the restaurant has a 30-foot mural featuring huge, colorful fruits; a long, curved bar that offers delicious fruit or vegetable juices; and an open kitchen with a wood-burning pizza oven.

Don't expect to find Buddhist monks dining here. This hip, sometimes celebrity-studded, vibrant restaurant features pop music instead of meditative chants. Nonetheless, it is also an eatery where you can relax and enjoy friendly and professional service.

The eclectic dinner menu contains thirty-one items, ranging from appetizers such as Beijing Vegetable Pot Stickers, filled with minced vegetables and complemented with soy-chili and peanut dipping sauces, to the delightful and very popular Brazillian Shellfish Stew (shellfish and whitefish cooked in a wood-burning oven and served with jasmine rice and topped with crispy plantains).

Other popular dinner entries are mussels steamed with white wine, lemongrass, shallots, kaffir lime, lime leaf, and cilantro; and the Wood Oven–Roasted Seasonal Vegetables drizzled with olive oil, balsamic vinegar, and herbs and served with whole roasted garlic cloves. The thick-crusted Get Shorty Pizza is always in demand (with grilled vegetables, Gorgonzola cheese, sautéed spinach, mushrooms, Yukon gold potatoes, and lots of roasted garlic).

The lunch menu has even more vegan selections than dinner. Favorites include the an Avocado PLT sandwich, with portobello mushrooms and eggless mayo on a multigrain bun, or the Crescent Trail Sandwich (roasted and grilled vegetables with hummus in house-made pita bread). The menu changes with the season, but a current favorite is the Wok-Smeared Sesame Spinach Salad with slivered green papaya, carrots, crispy wontons and a spicy Asian dressing.

Needless to say, the desserts here are exceptional. The selections change every three months, but they always include at least one vegan option, such as the Mango Crisp (fresh sliced mango baked in a light phyllo crust and served with lychee sorbet). A nice selection of organic wines is available, but for a more unusual experience try the fruit or vegetable juices.

Brazilian Shellfish Stew

Serves 4 as a main course

Co-owner Mark Caraluzzi credits this recipe to Peter Vazquez, the restaurant's chef. He adds that the stew is his and his wife's favorite seafood dish at Thyme Square.

"It's been on the menu since opening day, and its popularity has flourished through all the seasons. Whether the weather is hot or cold, the dish is satisfying and unique in flavor."

He adds that it is a simple dish to make at home. "We've made it at home on frequent occasions, and what makes it so simple is that the broth is prepared in advance and the seafood is simply poached in the broth.

"The basic recipe has a minimum of heat/spiciness to it. A hotter flavor can be achieved by adding additional sambal olek, which is essentially a red chili combination with spices."

STEW BASE

1 tablespoon canola oil

1/2 cup chopped onions

2 cloves garlic, minced

1 tomato, chopped

1 tablespoon chopped fresh cilantro

2 tablespoons minced fresh parsley

3 1/2 cups vegetable stock

4 cups light coconut milk

1 teaspoon salt

1/2 teaspoon sambal olek (red chili paste)

2 teaspoons cracked black pepper

Juice of 1/2 lemon

$1^1/2$ pounds mixed shellfish and firm whitefish, such as large shrimp, littleneck clams, mussels, sea bass, grouper, cod

Steamed basmati rice for serving

To make stew base: In a large, heavy saucepan over medium heat, heat oil and sauté onions for 5 minutes. Add garlic and sauté for 3 minutes. Add tomato, cilantro, parsley, and vegetable stock and simmer for 20 minutes.

Add all remaining stew base ingredients. Bring to a simmer and cook for 10 minutes. Use now, or let cool, cover, and refrigerate for up to 2 days.

If refrigerated, re-heat stew base in a large pot. Shell and devein shrimp. Scrub clams. Scrub and debeard mussels. Cut fish into 1-inch cubes. Add shellfish and fish, cover, and simmer for about 4 minutes, or until clams and mussels open, shrimp is pink, and fish is opaque throughout. Discard any mussels or clams that do not open.

Place a portion of rice in the center of a large shallow soup bowl. Arrange fish and shellfish around rice. Pour in enough broth to make a soup.

THE VEGETABLE GARDEN
11618 Rockville Pike
Rockville, Maryland 20852
301-468-9301

OPEN DAILY 11:30 A.M. TO 10 P.M.

Price: Moderate
Credit cards: AE, D, MC, V
Wheelchair accessible
No smoking
Alcohol: Beer and wine

The Vegetable Garden is not just another Chinese restaurant. This Rockville, Maryland, eatery specializes in vegetarian, vegan, and macrobiotic cuisine made from organically grown foods.

The inviting dining room is decorated with poster-sized prints of pristine vegetables. A small bar located at the back of the room is accented by odd-shaped gourds.

Patrons are always pleasantly surprised when one of the attentive wait staff brings a basket of whole-wheat sesame bread to the table. Other surprises include the exclusive use of bottled water, a choice of brown or white steamed rice, and the availability of fresh squeezed organic carrot, orange, grapefruit juice, and organic bottled apple juice.

The unique menu is illustrated with photographs and describes how each dish is cooked, what ingredients it contains, and which ingredients were grown organically and which conventionally. It also points out that organic low-sodium tamari soy sauce and little or no oil is used in meal preparation.

Voted one of the nation's ten great vegetarian restaurants by *Self* magazine, and one of the top thirty vegetarian restaurants by *Natural Living Magazine*, the Vegetable Garden specializes in "Buddhist cuisine that uses no animal products and no garlic."

The Vegetable Garden is a favorite restaurant for locals and D.C.-area vegetarians. One dish that keeps them coming back is the Kung Pao Tofu with peanuts and green peppers. Other favorites include appetizers such as Crispy Black Mushrooms, Moo-Shu Cilantro Roll, and Spinach Mini Knishes (which are also made with broccoli, green beans, or shiitake mushrooms). The Mesclun Salad contains thirty-six ingredients, thirty-three of which are varieties of greens and herbs.

Main course best-sellers include Eight-Treasure Eggplant (shiitake mushrooms, yellow squash, zucchini, red bell pepper, tofu, eggplant, lily bulbs, cashews, dried cranberries, and pine nuts, served with rice); Sesame-Vegi Chicken (organic tofu, wheat flour, carrot, asparagus, yellow squash, and sesame seeds); Veggie Duck with Vegetables in a Hot Pot; and the Cabbage Rolls Bamboo Raft.

Among the delicious desserts are Organic Carrot Cake, Kranberry Krunchy, Sesame Peanut Halvah, Rhubarb Pie, and Sweet Potato Pie.

Spaghetti Squash Patties

Serves 6 as a side dish

The Spaghetti Squash Patties are a "hands-down favorite" and a "delightful crowd pleaser," according to general manager George Zhong. He adds that the recipe is easy to make at home, and that it typifies the art of Chinese cooking, which emphasizes "the selection, blending, and harmonizing of texture, color, aroma, and taste."

1 spaghetti squash (about $2^1/2$ pounds), sliced

2 tablespoons organic whole-wheat flour

$1/2$ to 1 teaspoon sea salt

1 teaspoon finely chopped green onion (green portion only)

Leaving the skins on, steam the cut squash over boiling water in a covered pot for about 15 minutes. Let cool. Pull out flesh of squash and place in a large bowl. Add flour, green onions, and salt. If mixture is too dry, spray with water. If too liquid, add a little more flour.

Spray a large skillet with vegetable-oil cooking spray. Heat over medium heat. Using a scant $1/2$-cup measure, add 3 to 4 portions squash mixture to skillet. With a spatula or spoon, flatten to $1/4$ inch thick.

Continue to flip patties over until browned on each side, a total cooking time of about 6 minutes. Keep warm in a 200°F oven while cooking remaining squash mixture.

BELA VEGETARIAN RESTAURANT
68 Masonic Street
Northampton, Massachusetts 01060
413-586-8011

OPEN TUESDAY THROUGH SATURDAY NOON TO 8:45 P.M.

Price: Moderate
No credit cards
No wheelchair access
No smoking
Alcohol: BYO

Set on a quiet side street, Bela Vegetarian restaurant is a respite from Northhampton's busy main thoroughfare. Outdoor picnic seating in the summer amid flowers and English ivy makes this restaurant truly a delight for the taste buds as well as for the eyes.

Bela's, a small, cozy eatery located next to the local fire station, has been serving up vegetarian fare in the Pioneer Valley for more than seven years.

The restaurant's colorful walls feature a changing exhibition of artwork by local artists.

At Bela's the motto has long been, "Vegetarian does not mean boring!" And over the years it has successfully lived up to that standard, as a glance at the chalkboard menu will prove.

On any given day customers can be tempted by treats such as Indian dal (yellow split peas), seitan Filipino-style (with sautéed onions), polenta (with rich tomato or cream sauces), and another Italian-inspired dish called Raphael Pasta.

Favorites on the regular menu — utilizing organic ingredients when available — include the Harvest Burger, the Veggie Cutlet, and Beans of the Day. Desserts are either honey or sugar-sweetened, and either dairy or dairy-free.

Spicy Sesame Noodles

Serves 5 as an appetizer

When Spicy Sesame Noodles was briefly removed from the menu, Bela's customers begged for it until it was put back on. This spicy and succulent dish can either be served chilled as an appetizer or with a salad as a main course.

"We tend to do things the old-fashioned way," explains the restaurant. "A dash of this and a dash of that. The recipe provided is basic. We've provided the ingredients and we encourage you to experiment. All you need is a blender and a plate."

1 clove chopped garlic

1 teaspoon chopped ginger

1 to 3 Thai chilis (less depending on your tolerance)

$1/2$ cup smooth peanut butter

1 tablespoon sesame oil

$1/3$ cup vegetable stock (more if needed)

$1/8$ teaspoon red pepper flakes

salt and black pepper to taste

Cilantro (optional)

6 ounces cooked Chinese egg noodles

Place warm vegetable stock in blender.

Add all remaining ingredients and blend until smooth. Adjust seasoning. Cook noodles, preferably thin style. Chill.

Toss noodles in sauce before serving.

Sauce can be stored for 3 to 4 days in refrigerator.

INN SEASON CAFE
500 East Fourth Street
Royal Oak, Michigan 48067
248-547-7916

OPEN TUESDAY THROUGH THURSDAY 11:30 A.M. TO 9 P.M.; FRIDAY UNTIL 10 P.M.; SATURDAY NOON TO 10 P.M.

Price: Moderate
Credit cards: AE, MC, V
Wheelchair accessible
No smoking
No alcohol

Located a short walking distance from the heart of Royal Oak's antiques district, the Inn Season Cafe is the perfect stop for lunch or dinner after a day of shopping for time-worn treasures.

Gentle lighting from teardrop chandeliers, lace curtains at the windows, and fresh flowers on the tables all help to create a warm and cozy yet elegant atmosphere.

Old church pews serve as booths, and the chairs at the wooden tables are upholstered with colorful fabrics. A revolving art exhibit features works of local artists.

Since opening its doors more than 17 years ago, this vegetarian restaurant has built an outstanding reputation for not compromising quality and for its freshly prepared cuisine.

Ingredients are mostly organic, and some dishes can be prepared without dairy products on request. The creative and regional cuisine pays homage to old-world roots. Indian, Italian, Mexican, Japanese, and Middle Eastern dishes are prepared here in a traditional manner.

"This cuisine is prepared the old-fashioned way, without modern amenities like microwave ovens," George Vutetakis, owner and chef, states. "Our food caresses the taste buds. We believe that enjoying a meal on its own time is a basic necessity of life."

To start your meal, try the popular Brazilian Black Beans (a spread of spiced black beans and vegetables, served with corn bread made with organic cornmeal, roasted sweet red peppers, black olives, and ancho mole salsa).

Among the most popular entrées are the Famous Fourth Street Burger (a grain burger served with vegetable relish) and the Inn Season Salad (romaine lettuce, vegetables, chickpeas, sprouts, marinated onions, and nuts, served with a choice of sautéed tofu, low-fat cheese, soy cheese, or avocado).

Other favorites are Szechwan Stir-Fry (sautéed tofu with fresh ginger and a mild peanut sauce), and Tofu Arame (tofu with sea vegetables and kale). One of the most popular lunch dishes is whitefish from northern Canadian lakes, baked with sesame-Dijon sauce and served with brown rice and a vegetable.

Daily dinner specials include the Portobello Linguini (udon noodles with portobello mushrooms and a fresh basil sauce, served with garlic-herb toast) and the Moroccan dinner (a colorful, fragrant vegetable ragout, with whole spices and saffron, served with couscous, hot-spice oil, and freshly cooked flat bread with za'atar), an herb found in the Mediterranean, similar to marjoram. Several fresh fish entrées are also featured daily.

The Apple Crisp is a favorite on the dessert menu, and there is a nice selection of teas and organic coffees to go with it.

Stuffed Tomatoes Provençal

Serves 8 as a main course

Owner and chef George Vutetakis writes that Stuffed Tomato Provençal "is one of the most requested dinners we have served over the years. This preparation has been at the cafe since its inception. The rice mixture is derived from a vegetarian grape leaf stuffing that my grandmother would make especially for me. The sauce contains the herbs of Provence."

RICE STUFFING

2 tablespoons extra-virgin olive oil

1 garlic clove, minced

1 onion, diced

$1/2$ cup walnuts

4 cups fresh Italian tomatoes

1 tablespoon dried mint

1 tablespoon dried dill

1 bay leaf

$1/3$ cup pine nuts

$1/3$ cup dried currants

1 tablespoon ground nutmeg

1 cinnamon stick

1 tablespoon fresh lemon juice

1 teaspoon molasses

1 teaspoon salt

2 cups organic white basmati rice

1 cup water

8 large tomatoes

CREAM SAUCE

1 tablespoon olive oil

$1/4$ cup diced leek

1 garlic clove, minced

3 ounces white mushrooms, sliced

$3/4$ cup dry white wine

2 cups organic half-and-half

1^1/2 teaspoons oregano

^{1}/2 teaspoon marjoram

^{1}/2 teaspoon tarragon

^{1}/2 teaspoon thyme

^{1}/2 teaspoon basil

^{1}/2 teaspoon dill

CHEESE TOPPING

^{1}/2 cup plain natural yogurt or sour cream

1 cup (4 ounces) brick, jack, or mild Cheddar cheese

8 Niçoise or kalamata olives for garnish

Preheat oven to 375ºF. To make stuffing: In a large, heavy saucepan over medium heat, heat oil and sauté garlic and onion for 1 minute.

Add all remaining ingredients except rice and water. Stir to blend. Add rice and water and cook until deep holes form in mixture. Transfer to a baking dish, cover with aluminum foil, and bake for 15 minutes. Remove from oven but leave oven on. Uncover, remove bay leaf and cinnamon stick, and let sit until ready to stuff the tomatoes.

Blanch tomatoes in boiling water to cover for 15 seconds. Using a slotted spoon, transfer to a bowl of cold water to cool slightly. Drain. Cut off and reserve top, remove peel, and hollow out tomatoes, leaving a ^{1}/4-inch shell. Set aside.

To make sauce: In a large saucepan over medium heat, heat oil and sauté leek, garlic, and mushrooms until soft. Add white wine and cook to reduce by half. Add half-and-half and cook to reduce to consistency of gravy. Set aside and keep warm.

Fill the tomatoes with rice stuffing (you will have some left over) and place in baking pan.

Top with 1 teaspoon yogurt or sour cream, then 1 tablespoon cheese. Place lids on and cover pan with aluminum foil. Bake for 30 to 40 minutes, or until heated through and tender.

Place a bed of remaining stuffing on each plate and put a stuffed tomato on top. Ladle $1/4$ cup of cream sauce over tomato. Garnish center with an olive.

Three-Grain Risotto

Serves 4 to 6 as a main course

"Grains are the staff of life, and the grains in this recipe have provided sustenance over the centuries for millions of people. Quinoa was the mother grain of the Incas, and millet has long been a staple in Africa. Wild rice, an American grain, gives the dish a nutty flavor," says chef and owner George Vutetakis.

MUSHROOM STOCK
1 teaspoon extra-virgin olive oil
2 garlic cloves, minced
1 leek, thinly sliced crosswise
6 ounces white mushrooms, sliced
1 teaspoon ground nutmeg
1 cinnamon stick
1 bay leaf
$1/2$ cup dry white wine, preferably organic, or 1 tablespoon Dijon mustard
1 teaspoon tamari soy sauce
6 grinds black pepper
2 cups milk, half-and-half, or soy milk mixed with 1 teaspoon flour

WILD RICE
$1^1/4$ cups water
$1/2$ cup wild rice
1 bay leaf
1 teaspoon olive oil
1 tablespoon fresh lemon juice
1 cup organic millet
1 cup organic quinoa
2 cups water
2 teaspoons salt
1 teaspoon olive oil

Preheat oven to 375°F. To make stock: In a medium saucepan over medium heat, heat oil and sauté garlic, leek, mushrooms, nutmeg, cinnamon stick, and bay leaf for 30 seconds. Add wine or mustard, soy sauce, and pepper. Cook to reduce the wine by about half. If using Dijon, cook until leeks are tender.

Add milk, half-and-half, or soy milk mixture and simmer for 5 minutes. If using soy milk mixture, whisk until hot. Reserve half of this mixture.

To cook rice: In a small saucepan, bring $1^1/4$ cups water with salt to a boil, add rice, bay leaf, and olive oil, and bring to boil again. Transfer to a baking dish, cover with aluminum foil, and bake for 50 minutes. Set aside.

Rinse millet in a fine-meshed sieve. In a medium saucepan, bring 2 cups water and reserved stock to a boil. Transfer to baking dish. Add the quinoa and millet. Cover with aluminum foil and bake for 15 minutes. Remove from oven, toss with cooked wild rice, and serve with a spoonful of stock.

CAFE BRENDA
300 First Avenue North
Minneapolis, Minnesota 55401
1-800-949-0154

OPEN FOR LUNCH MONDAY THROUGH FRIDAY 11:30 A.M. TO 2 P.M.; DINNER MONDAY THROUGH FRIDAY 5:30 TO 9 P.M., SATURDAY UNTIL 10 P.M.

Price: Moderate
Credit cards: AE, MC, V
Wheelchair accessible
No smoking
Alcohol: Extensive wine list, beer

Located one mile from the University of Minnesota in a historic district of downtown Minneapolis, this upscale natural foods restaurant has won rave reviews from *Gourmet Magazine*, which describes it as "an extraordinary restaurant . . . meals are healthful, but uncompromising in taste."

Cafe Brenda is housed in a renovated warehouse with plenty of windows and high ceilings. Despite the warehouse setting, the space is warm and inviting and features contemporary decor.

The terra-cotta floors are softened with Oriental rugs, while the terra-cotta-colored walls are adorned with botanical prints. At dinner, white tablecloths and candlelight conjure up an intimate and romantic mood.

The restaurant has been at this location for 12 years, with a sister eatery now in its eighth year of operation in nearby St. Paul.

Daily seafood and vegetable specials are offered, along with an eclectic mix of vegetarian appetizers, sandwiches, and entrées. There is also an a la carte menu, as well as a special children's menu.

One of the restaurant's most popular specials is Croquettes of the Day (two sautéed grain, bean, and vegetable patties, topped with sauce and served with organic greens and vegetables). This special varies daily to reflect a different cuisine. For example, if the cuisine is Southern, diners can expect their croquettes to be accompanied with vegetables and Georgia-grown pecans. If Mediterranean cuisine is the choice of the day, the croquettes will be made of eggplant and accompanied with chickpeas.

So popular are Cafe Brenda's croquettes that the restaurant packages and markets them in supermarkets and natural foods stores throughout the Minneapolis/St. Paul area.

Another popular dish is Wisconsin Rainbow Trout (sautéed whole fresh fish, topped with a tangy East Indian mint sauce). All entrées are served with a basket of organic sourdough bread and home-made corn bread.

Popular appetizers include organic greens and the very special Chèvre Salad (goat cheese rolled in fresh herbs, marinated apricots, hazelnuts, and fresh fruits on a bed of organic greens, dressed with a mango-shallot vinaigrette).

The desserts use only maple syrup and honey as sweeteners. You *must* try the always-in-demand Chocolate Carrot Cake. Besides an extensive wine list, the cafe also offers an interesting selection of beers, including Pyramid Apricot Ale and Sierra Nevada Stout.

Butternut Squash and Vegetable Gratin
Topped with Roasted Walnuts and Gruyère Cheese

Serves 4 as a main course

Brenda Langton writes in *Cafe Brenda Cookbook* (Voyager Publishers) that the Butternut Squash and Vegetable Gratin topped with Walnuts and Gruyère Cheese is one of the first meals she makes when fall comes.

"I feel fortunate to have a good market where I can go and fill my trunk with a variety of squash from one of my favorite growers. . . . The gratin is nice served with wild rice, salad, and fresh bread."

1 butternut squash, seeded, peeled, and cut into $1/2$-inch-thick slices (see note)

Olive oil for brushing, plus 2 tablespoons

Salt to taste, plus $1/2$ teaspoon salt

Freshly ground pepper to taste, plus $1/2$ teaspoon pepper

6 garlic cloves, minced

2 cups sliced halved leeks (white portion only)

1 red bell pepper, seeded, deribbed, and julienned

9 ounces white or wild mushrooms, sliced

6 to 8 tomatoes, sliced

$1/4$ cup chopped minced fresh herbs such as basil, marjoram, parsley, rosemary, thyme, mint, sage

$1/4$ cup walnuts, toasted

1 cup (4 ounces) grated Gruyère cheese or soy cheese

In a 7-by-11-inch baking dish layer half of squash, mushrooms, leek mixture, tomatoes, herbs, $1/2$ teaspoon salt, $1/2$ teaspoon pepper, walnuts, and cheese. Repeat with remaining ingredients.

Cover with aluminum foil and bake for 30 minutes. Remove foil and bake for 10 minutes, or until lightly browned.

NOTE: CUT BULBOUS END OFF SQUASH. CUT SQUASH IN HALF AND CLEAN OUT SEEDS AND STRINGY PULP. CUT INTO SLICES AND PEEL EACH SLICE SEPARATELY. CUT FLESH INTO CHUNKS FOR COOKING.

Chickpea Pumpkin Soup

Serves 6 as a main course

Brenda says that Chickpea Pumpkin Soup, another recipe from her cookbook, is a popular fall favorite at her cafe. "This recipe uses chickpeas and oatmeal for a healthy, rich flavor. Serve the soup with bread and a salad for a very satisfying meal."

1 cup dried chickpeas

6 cups water

3 tablespoons vegetable oil

1 onion, coarsely chopped

1 small pumpkin, peeled, seeded, and cut into 1-inch pieces (5 to 6 cups)

5 cups water or vegetable stock

$1 1/2$ teaspoons salt

$1/2$ teaspoon dried thyme

$1/4$ cup rolled oats

Rinse and pick over chickpeas. Soak for at least 4 hours (or overnight if possible) in water to cover by several inches. Drain. In a soup pot, combine chickpeas and water. Bring to a boil. Reduce heat, cover, and simmer, until tender, 1 to $1^1/2$ hours.

In a soup pot over medium heat, heat oil and sauté onion until soft. Add pumpkin and sauté for 10 minutes. Add water or stock, salt, thyme, and rolled oats.

Cover pot, reduce heat, and simmer until pumpkin is tender, about 30 minutes. Add beans and continue cooking for 10 to 15 minutes. Serve now, while pumpkin is in chunks, or for a smoother soup, continue to cook until pumpkin falls apart.

NOTE: CUT OFF TOP AND BOTTOM OF PUMPKIN SO IT WILL SIT WELL ON A CUTTING SURFACE. WITH A LARGE, SHARP KNIFE, CUT DOWN SIDES TO REMOVE PEEL FROM TOP TO BOTTOM. CUT PUMPKIN IN HALF AND CLEAN OUT SEEDS AND STRINGY PULP.

THE NEW BLACK DOG CAFE
138 West Broadway
Missoula, Montana 59802
406-542-1138

OPEN MONDAY THROUGH FRIDAY 11:30 A.M. TO 9 P.M., SATURDAY 5:30 TO 10 P.M.

Price: Moderate
No credit cards
Wheelchair accessible
No smoking
No alcohol

Pull into a parking space in front of The New Black Dog Cafe on a summer day and the huge planter that runs the length of the restaurant will be overflowing with Montana state wildflowers. Inside, the cafe's decor is casual, cheerful, and as colorful as the wildflowers outside the restaurant's two large front windows.

The cafe exudes a casual, modern atmosphere, and artwork by local artists offers a colorful backdrop to the food. Co-owner Kris Love runs this eatery with partner Larry Evans.

The cafe is located in a shopping center near the heart of the city's downtown area, and it's popular with local residents as well as students from nearby University of Montana. It is the only vegetarian restaurant in the area.

The food here is organic (when available), fresh, and delicious. Daily lunch and dinner specials are offered, along with a full-course menu featuring soups, salads, sandwiches, entrées, and desserts. Almost everything on the premises is made from scratch.

Favorites at the cafe include the Smoked Tempeh Salad, Marinated Eggplant Sandwich, Potato Gordas, and the soups. The Skordalia (Greek garlic dip) is a tasty addition to salads and sandwiches. For dessert, don't miss the Chocolate Chip Pound Cake.

Skordalia (Greek Garlic Dip)

Makes about 3 cups

Kris and Larry chose the Skordalia (greek garlic dip) as one of the house favorite. "It's very simple, delicious, and intense. It is very popular with our customers and truly a delight for garlic-lovers.

"The simplicity of it makes it adaptable to individual tastes, and all the ingredients are probably in your kitchen right now."

$5^1/_2$ cups cubed coarse whole-wheat bread
$1^1/_2$ cups diced boiled potatoes
$^1/_2$ cup extra-virgin olive oil
$^1/_4$ cup rice vinegar
4 to 6 tablespoons minced garlic
1 tablespoon salt
$^1/_3$ to 1 cup water
Kalamata olives for garnish
Warm pita wedges for dipping

In a blender or food processor, in batches if necessary, combine bread, potatoes, oil, vinegar, garlic, and salt. Process for a few seconds to mix. With machine running, add water to make a mixture the consistency of oatmeal, then process for a few minutes until smooth.

Serve at room temperature or slightly chilled. Top with olives and serve with pita wedges.

CAFE CHIMES
Main Street, Norcross Place
North Conway, New Hampshire 03860
603-356-5500

Open daily 7 a.m. to 4 p.m.; dinner 5 to 9 p.m. in summer

Price: Inexpensive
No credit cards
No wheelchair access
No smoking
No alcohol

Nestled in the White Mountains of New Hampshire, Cafe Chimes has been a popular local eatery and meeting place since 1990. It is the only vegetarian restaurant in the Mount Washington Valley.

Located on North Conway's Main street, the restaurant's colorful vegetable-and-fruit-laced archway leads guests downstairs to a delightful cafe that is, according to the original owner Kathy Etter, "the kind of place that nourishes the body and the soul."

Etter is not only the restaurant's owner, she is also an expert on natural foods cooking and writes articles on nutrition and health for the local paper. "Our mission at Cafe Chimes is to bring consciousness to our eating habits and to the environment," she says.

In addition to dining here, if you have six weeks to spare you can sign up for a cooking class that explores the "whys and ways of a vegetarian lifestyle."

The menu lists a wide variety of healthful gourmet vegetarian fare. There are soups, sandwiches, quiches, pizzas, grain casseroles, daily specials, and nutrient-rich homemade desserts and breads. A salad bar is also available, and organically grown produce is used whenever possible. The cafe grinds wheat berries daily to create the unique whole-wheat bread that is a regional favorite.

For first-time visitors, Kathy suggests the Cafe Chimes Sampler Plate, consisting of a "cup of the gourmet soup of the day, a piece of whole-wheat bread, a portion of our baked grain-and-veggie casserole, hummus on a bed of lettuce, and a salad topped with creamy tahini dressing."

You might also want to try the low-fat, nutrient-rich desserts made with no dairy products, eggs, or refined sugar. Whole-wheat, grain-sweetened cookies and the Cafe Chimes Granola Bars are best-sellers.

Temptation Turkish Pilaf

Serves 4 to 6 as a side dish

"I selected the Temptation Turkish Pilaf because it is so wholesome and delicious," Kathy states. "The wonderful ethnic flavor of this dish is sure to tempt any palate." She adds that "the Outrageous Orange-Tahini Sauce is an easy and fun sauce that will put a smile on any face."

2 tablespoons olive oil
1 onion, chopped
4 celery stalks, diced
$1/2$ teaspoon ground allspice
$1/2$ teaspoon ground coriander

$1/2$ teaspoon ground cinnamon

2 cups white basmati rice, washed

3 cups water

Pinch of salt

1 cup dried currants

$1/2$ cup slivered almonds

In a pot over medium heat, heat oil and sauté onion until golden. Add celery and spices and sauté for 3 minutes. Add rice, water, salt, and currants. Cover and simmer for 45 minutes. Do not peek! Let sit for a few minutes, then fluff with a fork and serve, garnished with almonds.

Outrageous Orange-Tahini Sauce

Makes about $1^1/2$ cups

Serve this as you would a soy sauce — on rice dishes — or as a flavor enhancer for many main courses such as fish dishes.

1 small onion, chopped

$1/2$ cup tahini

1 garlic clove

$1/2$ cup tamari soy sauce

1 teaspoon dried oregano, or 1 tablespoon fresh oregano

2 tablespoons honey

$1/2$ cup frozen orange juice concentrate

In a blender, combine all ingredients and puree until smooth. Store in an airtight container in the refrigerator.

Very Vegetarian Chili

Serves 4 to 6 as a main course

2 cups boiling water

1 cup textured vegetable protein (TVP), crumbled

1 cup bulgur wheat

2 tablespoons olive oil

3 celery stalks, diced

4 garlic cloves, crushed

2 onions, finely chopped

3 carrots, finely chopped

2 green bell peppers, seeded, deribbed, and diced

2 teaspoons dried basil

3 tablespoons chili powder

2 tablespoons ground cumin

$1/8$ teaspoon cayenne pepper

2 cups cooked kidney beans

Juice of $1/2$ lemon

3 tablespoons tamari soy sauce

2 cups tomato sauce

Miso to taste

In a large bowl, combine boiling water, TVP, and bulgur. Cover and set aside. In a large skillet over medium heat, heat olive oil and sauté celery, garlic, and onions in oil until onions are translucent. Add carrots, peppers, basil, chili powder, cumin, and cayenne. Sauté a few more minutes, adding a little water if needed.

Combine TVP mixture, beans, and vegetables in a large pot. Add lemon juice, tamari, and tomato sauce. Simmer for approximately 45 to 60 minutes. Add miso and serve.

Dairy-Free Mushroom Stroganoff

Serves 4 to 6 as a main course

1 pound firm tofu, cubed

Juice of 1 lemon

2 tablespoons canola oil

$1/2$ cup tahini

1 tablespoon sesame oil

1 onion, finely chopped

1 garlic clove, minced

16 ounces white mushrooms, sliced

1 teaspoon paprika

$1^1/2$ teaspoons minced fresh thyme, or $1/2$ teaspoon dried thyme

1 tablespoon dried dill, or 3 tablespoons fresh

2 tablespoons fresh parsley, chopped

2 tablespoons tamari soy sauce

Cooked udon noodles for serving

In a blender, combine tofu, lemon juice, oil, and tahini and puree until smooth. Set aside. In a large skillet over medium heat, heat sesame oil and sauté onion and garlic until tender, about 5 minutes. Add mushrooms, paprika, thyme, dill, parsley, and tamari. Add tofu mixture. Mix with udon and serve.

PARK AND ORCHARD
240 Hackensack Street
East Rutherford, New Jersey 07072
201-939-9292

OPEN FOR DINNER MONDAY 5 TO 10 P.M. AND SATURDAY 4:45 TO 10 P.M.; CONTINUOUS SERVICE TUESDAY THROUGH FRIDAY NOON TO 10 P.M.; SUNDAY 2 P.M. TO 9 P.M.

Price: Expensive
All major credit cards
Wheelchair accessible
Smoking: Restricted section
Alcohol: Full bar

Park and Orchard has been favorably reviewed by every major magazine and newspaper in the state and beyond. It was voted the best restaurant in northern New Jersey by readers of *New Jersey Magazine*, and is listed by the *Zagat Survey* as one of the top five restaurants in the state.

But despite such hoopla, it remains a casual, comfortable place to dine — and the decor is still reminiscent of the old sheet metal plant that the building once was.

Situated not far from New York City, and close to the Meadowlands sports complex (home of the New York Giants and other teams), the decor is "art deco/industrial," according to co-owner and chef Buddy Gebhardt: high ceilings, a cavernous dining area, and relatively little on the walls.

This huge eatery can accommodate up to 180 people, and because of its popularity, on some nights it does. Gebhardt cautions that there is sometimes a long wait to get seated, so call to get on the advanced waiting list.

Park and Orchard draws diners from around the world, attracted to this somewhat off-the-beaten-path location outside of Manhattan by its fabulous culinary reviews.

In fact, according to a recent article in *American Express Magazine*, Park and Orchard has fewer local diners and more out-of-towners than most dining establishments, including many of the equally famous ones located in the heart of the nearby Big Apple.

"We have more people traveling here from out of the area than from town," quips Gebhardt, who runs the restaurant with his brother, Ken, "because they know a good thing when they read about it."

Specials to be found on the menu include Stuffed Acorn Squash (squash, onions, sweet potatoes, carrots, apples, and raw cashew nuts), and Ethel Gebhardt's Rice Pudding, which is "like no other rice pudding on this side of the earth."

Also quite popular is Shepherd's Casserole (rice, pinto beans, and enchilada sauce, topped with cheese), Black Bean Stir-Fry, and Wheatless-Dairyless Lasagna. Blue Corn Ravioli is also a treat, as is Cajun Vegetarian Meat Loaf. The eclectic menu also features chicken, fish, quail, and ostrich entrées for nonvegetarians.

"We're a natural foods restaurant, and our fowl have not been abused with injections of antibiotics or hormones — they're naturally fed and you can taste the difference," Gebhardt explains.

Cajun Meat Loaf with Chili Sauce

Serves 4 to 6 as a main course

"The Cajun Meat Loaf with Chili Sauce is the most popular vegetarian dish we serve here," says Gebhardt. "It smells just like meat.

"There are a lot of places that make vegetarian dishes like this one, but they're all kind of the same. This one you can't find anywhere but here. This is our own recipe, like our stuffed cabbage and stuffed peppers. This meat loaf is a copy of what I was brought up to eat by my mother — without the meat.

"Believe me, you'll think you were eating something that has meat in it. We have had Polish chefs working on this dish a long time to perfect it."

$1/2$ cup vegetable oil

1 cup long-grain brown rice

7 cups water

$2/3$ cup dried lentils

$1^1/2$ teaspoons salt

2 cups finely diced onions

1 cup finely chopped celery

4 jalapeno chilies, minced (optional)

1 cup finely diced green bell pepper

1 tablespoon minced garlic

1 cup chopped pecans

$1/2$ cup sesame seeds

$1/2$ teaspoon ground pepper

Pinch of white pepper (optional)

2 cups textured vegetable protein (TVP)

9 eggs

1 cup tomato juice

$1/4$ cup soy sauce

4 cups (1 pound) shredded Cheddar cheese

CHILI SAUCE

$1/4$ cup vegetable oil

1 onion, chopped

1 green bell pepper, seeded, deribbed, finely chopped

1 celery stalk, finely diced

2 jalapeno chilies, minced

32 ounces canned Italian tomatoes, drained and chopped

$1/2$ teaspoon ground coriander

1 heaping teaspoon ground cumin

Salt to taste

BARBECUE SAUCE

1 cup tomato sauce

$1/2$ teaspoon liquid smoke (optional)

$1/4$ cup sugar

$1/4$ cup cider vinegar

$1/4$ cup tomato paste

To make chili sauce: In a medium, heavy saucepan over medium heat, heat oil and sauté onion until translucent. Add pepper, celery, and jalapenos and sauté until tender. Add tomatoes and spices and cook for 10 minutes. Add salt. Set aside.

In a medium, heavy saucepan over low heat, heat up $1/4$ cup oil and cook rice, stirring constantly, until golden.

Add 3 cups water and cook uncovered until rice is tender about 30 minutes. Set aside.

In a medium saucepan, combine lentils, remaining 4 cups water, and $1/2$ teaspoon salt. Bring to a boil, reduce heat, cover, and cook until al dente, about 30 minutes. Drain and set aside.

Preheat oven to 275ºF. In a large skillet over medium heat, heat remaining $1/4$ cup oil and sauté half of onions until brown. Add remaining onions, celery, chilies, and green pepper and cook until tender, about 5 minutes.

Stir in remaining 1 teaspoon salt, garlic, nuts, sesame seeds, ground pepper, TVP, and barbecue sauce. Let cool. Beat eggs with tomato juice and add to mixture.

Add soy sauce and mix to blend all ingredients. Let sit for 5 minutes. Taste TVP; if crunchy, add a little water and let sit another 5 minutes.

Blend in cheese, form into a loaf shape, and place in a baking dish. Cover with aluminum foil and bake for 1 hour, or until firm.

Serve hot, cut into slices, with chili sauce or ketchup.

CAFE PASQUAL'S
121 Don Gaspar
Santa Fe, New Mexico 87501
505-983-9340

OPEN FOR BREAKFAST AND LUNCH MONDAY THROUGH SATURDAY 7 A.M. TO 3 P.M., SUNDAY 8 A.M TO 2 P.M.; DINNER DAILY 6 TO 10:30 P.M.

Price: Moderate to expensive
Credit cards: AE, MC, V
Wheelchair accessible
No smoking
Alcohol: Beer and wine

Cafe Pasqual's, a Santa Fe classic well known for its authentic Southwestern natural foods cuisine, is a festive, bustling corner cafe located one block off the historic plaza at the end of the Santa Fe trail.

Done up in the architectural style of Old Mexico, the restaurant's walls blaze with murals by Oaxacan painter Leovigildo Martinez.

The cafe is renowned for its breakfasts, and even people who claim never to touch eggs can't seem to resist trying the breakfast specialty, Huevos Matulenos (a hearty Yucatan breakfast of two over-easy eggs on blue corn tortillas, with black beans, topped with sautéed bananas, feta cheese, early peas, roasted-jalapeno salsa, and green chilies).

The dishes for lunch and dinner are equally as tempting. Locally grown fruits and vegetables are used here whenever possible. A best-seller is Napo's Pupusa (a corn masa cake with sweet peppers and onion escabèche). Other popular entrées are the Chicken Mole Puebla with Mexican rice, squash tamale, and corn tortillas, and the Grilled Salmon Burrito with black beans, herbed goat cheese, and cucumber salsa.

The desserts also have a Southwestern flavor, such as the Roasted Piñon Ice Cream with Caramel Sauce.

Corn Cakes with Calabacitas and Queso Blanco Salsa

Serves 6 as a main course

Chef Katharine Kagel says that Corn Cakes with Calabacitas and Queso Blanco Salsa is beloved by vegetarian and nonvegetarians alike. "Using natural ingredients, this recipe can be easily prepared at home and appreciated for its warm, fresh flavors and wholesome appeal."

This dish was inspired by the Southwest's classic corn and squash sauté. "The white cheese salsa is essentially the chile con queso of Old Mexico, but made with ingredients available north of the border." These corn cakes can be enjoyed as an appetizer or as a lunch or brunch main course. This recipe is from Kagel's *Cafe Pasqual's Cookbook* (Chronicle Books).

QUESO BLANCO SALSA
4 tablespoons unsalted butter
1 white onion, chopped
5 Roma (plum) tomatoes, peeled and chopped
4 fresh mild green chilies such as New Mexico or Anaheim, roasted, peeled,
and chopped, or 4 canned green chilies, rinsed and chopped
1 red bell pepper, seeded, deribbed, and diced
1 yellow bell pepper, seeded, deribbed, and diced

$^1/4$ teaspoon salt

$^1/4$ teaspoon ground pepper

$^1/2$ cup half-and-half

8 ounces cream cheese, cut into small pieces

$^1/2$ teaspoon cayenne pepper

CORN CAKES

$^1/3$ cup finely diced red bell pepper

1 cup fresh or thawed frozen corn kernels

3 eggs

$^3/4$ cup milk

$^1/2$ cup all-purpose flour

$^1/3$ cup stone-ground yellow cornmeal

2 tablespoons unsalted butter, melted and cooled

1 teaspoon salt

2 dashes of Tabasco sauce

$^1/2$ to 1 teaspoon cayenne pepper

$^1/4$ cup finely chopped green onions, including some green portions

$^1/4$ cup fresh cilantro leaves, chopped

3 tablespoons grated Parmesan cheese

Melted butter for cooking

CALABACITAS

2 tablespoons butter, melted

2 cups fresh or thawed frozen corn kernels

1 cup finely diced red bell pepper

1 cup finely diced zucchini

2 poblano chilies, stemmed, seeded, and finely chopped

Fresh cilantro sprigs for garnish

To make salsa: In a large skillet, melt butter over medium heat. When butter sizzles, add onion and sauté until translucent, about 7 minutes. Add tomatoes, chilies, red and yellow bell peppers, salt, and pepper. Cook for 10 minutes, stirring frequently.

Reduce heat and add half-and-half, stirring well. When heated through, add cream cheese. Cook, stirring frequently, until cheese melts and mixture is thick, about 12 minutes.

Stir in cayenne pepper and remove from heat. Let cool, cover, and refrigerate until 30 minutes before serving (you may prepare salsa up to 3 days in advance).

Just before serving, reheat salsa over gently simmering water; stir frequently to prevent scorching. Adjust seasoning to taste with cayenne.

To make corn cakes: In a blender or food processor, combine bell pepper, corn, eggs, milk, flour, cornmeal, butter, and salt. Process for about 30 seconds.

Transfer mixture to a large bowl and stir in Tabasco sauce, cayenne, green onions, cilantro, and Parmesan. Cover and let stand for 30 minutes at room temperature.

Preheat the oven to 250ºF. Heat a 7-inch nonstick crepe pan over medium heat. Brush pan with melted butter. When butter sizzles, ladle 3 or 4 tablespoons batter into center of pan, then tilt and swirl pan to spread the batter thinly over pan's surface.

Cook until lightly browned on the bottom, about 2 minutes. Flip cake and cook until second side browns slightly, about 1 minute. Slide cake out onto a plate and cover with a square of waxed paper. Place in oven to keep warm. Repeat to make 6 cakes in all, brushing pan with butter as needed and stacking them on top of each other on plate. Cakes may be cooked up to 1 hour before serving.

To make calabacitas: Heat a medium skillet over medium heat. Brush pan with melted butter. When it sizzles, add all remaining ingredients.

Cook, shaking pan to rearrange ingredients frequently, until vegetables are just heated through and slightly softened, 3 to 4 minutes.

Place warm corn cakes on individual plates and spoon one sixth of calabacitas mixture on half of each cake. Fold other half over to form a half-moon. Ladle warm salsa over all. Garnish with cilantro sprigs.

BACHUE
36 West 21st Street
New York, New York 10010
212-229-0870

OPEN MONDAY THROUGH FRIDAY 8 A.M. TO 10:30 P.M., SATURDAY 10 A.M. TO 10:30 P.M., SUNDAY 11 A.M.
TO 7 P.M.

Price: Moderate
Credit cards: AE, D, DC, MC, V
Wheelchair accessible
No smoking
No alcohol

Bachue (pronounced bah-chu-WAY) is unique among natural foods restaurants, because it features South American vegetarian fare.

Co-owner Libardo Loiazo and his partner, Gabriel Vasquez, are from Colombia, and they named their cozy eatery in the heart of Manhattan's trendy photo district after the Chibcha people's (a native tribe of Columbia) legendary goddess.

Bachue honors the ancient indigenous tradition of eating foods prepared with care and respect. The food is healthy and of gourmet quality and the prices are reasonable (for New York City).

"Our primary commitment is quality, freshness, wholeness, and flavor," states Loiazo. "Every meal is well balanced, nutritious, and delicious."

There are a dozen tables here — many of them occupied by photographers and their models. The walls are exposed brick, hung with block cuts of cutesy "monsters."

The restaurant, which opened in 1994, features dishes ranging from whole-grain tacos and Tofu-Vegetable Lasagna to brown-rice nori rolls and the ever-popular Chickpea Crepes. The meals are dairy-free, low in fat, high in fiber, and cholesterol-free. Only filtered water and stainless steel cookware are used.

A good start to a meal here is one or two of the terrific appetizers on the menu such as Yuca with Garlic and Olive Oil or nori rolls with pickled ginger wasabi and dipping sauce.

Among the best-selling plates are the South American Twist (a tantalizing blend of sautéed seasonal vegetables and potatoes wrapped in an herbed chickpea crepe, and draped with an onion-mushroom sauce), and Spirits Alive (a crispy corn or whole-wheat tortilla piled high with flavor-packed refried beans, shredded lettuce, carrots, beets, sprouts, radishes, and jicama, topped with tofu sour cream and an avocado slice and served with home-made green salsa).

A favorite sandwich is the Burrito Bandito (a corn or whole-wheat tortilla wrapped around refried beans, rice, roasted red peppers, avocados, coleslaw, and salsa, topped with tofu sour cream and served with a salad).

Another favorite is the Sandwich for All Seasons (your choice of tofu or tempeh cooked in zesty marinade, served on sourdough whole-grain bread with roasted peppers, lettuce, cucumbers, sprouts, carrots, and beets with a side of house-made sauerkraut and tomatillo salsa). There are also daily specials, so ask your waiter what the selection is for today.

For dessert-lovers, the tempting treats, all made with maple syrup, barley malt, or rice syrup, include Strawberry Mango Crisp and Blueberry-Apple Pie.

Freshly squeezed organic juices, soy milk, herbal teas, organic coffee, and natural sodas are also available.

Chickpea Crepes

Serves 4 to 6 as a main course

According to the restaurant, "The Chickpea Crepes is our biggest seller, and everybody loves this dish. This crepe is dairy-free, with no eggs or animal products. Gabriel Vasquez, co-owner of the cafe, created this recipe."

CREPES

1 cup whole-wheat pastry flour

1 cup chickpea flour

$1/2$ cup arrowroot

$1/4$ teaspoon sea salt

Pinch of white pepper

1 teaspoon minced fresh basil, parsley, or thyme

$1/3$ cup soy milk or rice milk

FILLING

1 teaspoon olive oil

1 large onion, diced

2 garlic cloves, minced

3 boiling potatoes, finely diced

1 carrot, finely diced

1 large tomato, finely diced

4 ounces shiitake mushrooms, sliced

2 rhubarb stalks, sliced

4 ounces English peas, shelled

$1/2$ bunch asparagus, trimmed and cut into $1/4$-inch slices

Tamari soy sauce to taste

To make crepes: In a blender, combine all ingredients except oil and blend until smooth.

Lightly oil a nonstick 7-inch crepe pan and heat over medium heat. Add batter and move in a circular motion until bottom is totally covered. Cook until lightly browned, then turn and cook on second side. Crepes may be stacked with aluminum foil or waxed paper. Keep warm in oven.

To make filling: In a large skillet over medium heat, heat oil and sauté onion, garlic, potatoes, and carrots until onion is translucent, about 3 minutes. Add tomato, mushrooms, rhubarb, peas, and asparagus and sauté for about 3 minutes, or until vegetables are crisp-tender. Add tamari and sauté for 1 minute. Put desired amount of filling in crepe, roll up, and serve.

HANGAWI
12 East 32nd Street
New York, New York 10016
212-213-0077

OPEN FOR LUNCH MONDAY THROUGH FRIDAY NOON TO 3 P.M.; FOR DINNER 5 TO 10:30 P.M.; SATURDAY 1 P.M. TO 11 P.M., SUNDAY TO 10 P.M.

Price: Expensive
Credit cards: AE, DC, MC, V
No wheelchair access
No smoking
Alcohol: Asian and Western beer and wine

This unique restaurant, which offers traditional Korean vegetarian cuisine won top vegetarian restaurant of the year kudos in the *Zagat Survey 1997* of the best New York City restaurants. The year before, HanGawi scored a near-perfect rating in the same survey.

The restaurant's ambiance is summed up in a recent *New York Times* review: "The air is filled with music as fresh as the wind whispering through branches in a remote mountain forest.

"Then it drops until it has turned into the melodic sound of water rushing over rocks. Slippers pad reverently across pine floors and servers kneel to place lacquered dishes on low tables. Wooden spoons slide from scarlet silk bags. Fragrant clouds of steam waft into the serene room as lids are lifted from hot stone bowls."

The *Zagat Survey* is equally flattering. It describes HanGawi's menu as one that "bursts with sublime culinary surprises of roots and greens. . . ."

Meals are eaten on low tables with cushions to sit on. There is a hollow space below each table so guests do not have to sit cross-legged. The decor is quite elegant, with the dark wood of the tables and the light wood of the floors blending harmoniously. The richly colored cushions accent the muted colors of the curved walls and ceiling.

HanGawi is an oasis of peace and quiet in a city known for its high rises and equally towering stress levels. Think of this eatery more as a spa than a restaurant, and you'll get the idea.

If you want to sample a good selection of the out-of-this world menu, try the Chef's Special Emperor's Meal or the HanGawi Emperor's Meal. Both feature enormous servings of the organically raised foods the restaurant is famous for.

Main courses vary seasonally. One recent Emperor's Meal consisted of two starters, three appetizers (a mini potato leek and mung bean pancake, a tofu sandwich with a lemon surprise, and crispy mushrooms in sweet and sour sauce), and a choice of entrées (either Vegetarian Stone Bowl Rice or Shiitake Mushrooms with Scallions in Garlic Sauce.)

The entrées come with "nine kinds of grain rice," kimchi, mountain roots and vegetables, and bean paste soup. The marvelous desserts go well with the unusual teas brewed here, including red ginseng, date paste, and mushroom.

HanGawi, by the way, is the name of the full August moon, a time when glutinous rice with five beans is served.

Tofu Sandwich with Cucumber Salad and Soy Sauce

Serves 1 as a main course

From owner Terri Choi comes a recipe that has been passed down in Chois' family for generations. "The Tofu Sandwich with Cucumber Salad and Soy Sauce is an excellent vegetarian dish because it is crispy and tasty. The oyster mushroom and tofu filling tastes like a meat filling."

Mushroom-Tofu Filling

4 ounces oyster mushrooms, finely chopped

1 teaspoon minced green onion

1 teaspoon minced leeks

$1/2$ teaspoon minced carrot

1 teaspoon potato starch

$1/2$ teaspoon Asian sesame oil

$1/4$ teaspoon ground pepper

$1/4$ teaspoon salt

1 teaspoon silken tofu, mashed

$1/2$ teaspoon sesame seeds

$1/2$ teaspoon minced garlic

$1/2$ teaspoon ginger juice

Two $1/2$-inch-thick slices extra-firm square tofu

Soybean oil for frying

Tempura Batter Mix

1 cup flour

$1/8$ cup cornstarch

$1/8$ teaspoon baking soda

$1/4$ cup rice powder

1 to $1 1/2$ cup cold water

Dipping Sauce

1 tablespoon soy sauce

2 teaspoons water

1 teaspoon minced green onion

$1/2$ teaspoon Asian sesame oil

Cucumber Salad (recipe follows)

To make filling: In a small bowl, mix all ingredients together.

Cut each square of firm tofu in half (horizontally) and fill with tofu filling.

Making the tempura batter: Mix flour, cornstarch, baking soda, and rice powder. Add water a little at a time and stir until thick and starchy. Dip tofu sandwich in batter until well coated.

In a Dutch oven or deep fryer heat $1/4$ inch of soybean oil to 180ºF and deep-fry the tofu 3 to 4 minutes. Using a slotted metal spatula, transfer tofu to paper towels to drain.

To make the dipping sauce: In a very small bowl, combine all ingredients. To serve, cut each tofu piece in half diagonally. Serve dipping sauce and salad alongside.

Cucumber Salad

Serves 1 as a side dish

1 oriental cucumber (kirby), finely sliced
$1/4$ teaspoon salt
$1/2$ teaspoon Asian sesame oil
$1/4$ teaspoon chili powder
$1/4$ teaspoon sugar
$1/4$ teaspoon ground pepper
$1/4$ teaspoon vinegar

In a small bowl, combine all ingredients and mix well.

MOOSEWOOD RESTAURANT
DeWitt Building
215 North Cayuga Street
Ithaca, New York 14850
607-273-9610

Open for lunch Monday through Saturday 11:30 a.m. to 2 p.m., snacks 2 to 4 p.m. Fall through spring: Open for dinner Sunday through Thursday 5:30 to 8:30 p.m., Friday and Saturday to 9 p.m. Summer: Open for dinner Sunday through Thursday 5:30 to 9 p.m., Friday and Saturday 6 to 9:30 p.m.

Price: Moderate
Credit cards: MC, V
Wheelchair accessible
No smoking
Alcohol: Full bar

With its emphasis on natural foods cuisine, Moosewood Restaurant has operated successfully in Ithaca for more than 23 years. The restaurant has become a legend among vegetarian restaurants, and is acclaimed as a driving force in the world of creative vegetarian cooking.

Interestingly, it is a collectively owned business. Currently, twenty members share management duties and the everyday tasks of cooking and serving along with a "corps of talented, dedicated employees who contribute to the smooth operation of the business."

Nestled amid the rolling hills, farms, and spectacular gorges of New York's Finger Lakes, the town of Ithaca is the home to both Cornell University and Ithaca College and is situated at the southern end of Cayuga Lake.

The restaurant is located in the city's downtown area in a renovated historic brick school building that now houses stores and apartments. Mostly it's locals — from neighborhood businessmen to students — who frequent Moosewood, but the popularity of the restaurant's cookbooks draws the tourists from around the world.

There's nothing fancy about the restaurant's interior: Rows of tables with wooden chairs crowd a pair of rooms that still have a classroom feel to them. "Homey" is a good way to describe the overall effect.

The exterior of the restaurant is also nondescript. In fact, many people seeking out this famed vegetarian eatery often drive right past it, believing it to be a workshop or some other institutional space.

The adventurous chefs at Moosewood prepare different offerings every day and at every meal. In fact, if you'd like to know what's on the menu for lunch, call the restaurant after 9 A.M. the same day and they'll let you know. What's cooking for dinner is decided by 3 P.M., and again, a phone call is advisable.

While all this may sound a bit improvisational, there's a method to such madness: It allows Moosewood's chefs to take advantage of the freshest seasonal produce available (organic when possible).

The natural foods cuisine served here is simply delicious. Some favorite lunch items include Lasagna, Middle Eastern Salad Plate (tabbouleh, hummus, "tofulafels" — falafels made with tofu — rice stuffed grape leaves and feta on a bed of fresh greens with pita and a cup of soup), and Sweet and Sour Vegetables with Tofu (carrots, red and green bell peppers, mushrooms, zucchini, green beans, water chestnuts, and pineapple in a tangy sauce served on rice and topped with green onion and cashews — served with a tossed salad).

Among the popular dinner entrées are Fresh Spinach Ravioli (with a rich hazelnut pesto and chopped fresh tomatoes, topped with grated Parmesan cheese) and Cauliflower-Green Pea Curry (a mélange of vegetables in a spicy and satisfying sauce served on coconut rice, topped with toasted cashews and currents and served with tomato chutney and lentil dal).

Thursday through Sunday, a fish entrée is found on the menu. Sunday is "ethnic foods night," when the chefs prepare dishes from a particular country or region.

Also in great demand are the fresh soups, salads, and pita sandwiches. The menu also features an extensive array of herbal teas, juices, and creative desserts, many of which are dairyless. You might also wish to try the excellent New York State wines and the regionally brewed Yuengling beer, ale, and porter.

Savory Indian Sweet Potatoes

Serves 2 as a main course, 4 as a side dish

"Creamy, sweet, and spicy" is the way Moosewood's chefs describe the Savory Indian Sweet Potatoes. "When you're baking sweet potatoes for another meal, put in a few extras so that later you'll have some prebaked for this dish. Serve on plain rice or golden basmati rice topped with a fresh tomato salsa or with a mango or peach chutney and, if desired, with a dollop of nonfat yogurt."

2 large sweet potatoes
1 cup diced onions
$1/3$ cup water, unsweetened apple juice, or orange juice
3 garlic cloves, minced or pressed
$1^1/2$ tablespoons grated fresh ginger
2 teaspoons ground cumin
1 small fresh green chili, seeded and minced
$2/3$ cup diced red and/or green bell pepper
3 tablespoons Neufchâtel (low-fat cream cheese)
$1^1/2$ tablespoons fresh lemon juice
$1/2$ cup fresh or slightly thawed frozen green peas
Salt and freshly ground pepper to taste

Bake sweet potatoes at 400°F for about 1 hour, or until tender. While potatoes bake, combine onions and water or juice in a medium saucepan. Cover and simmer until onions soften, about 5 minutes. Add garlic, ginger, cumin, chili, and bell pepper. Cover and simmer until pepper is tender, about 5 minutes. Remove from heat. Cut Neufchâtel into small pieces and stir it into hot vegetable mixture to melt. Set aside.

Cut sweet potatoes in half lengthwise. Hold each potato half with a heavy towel or mitt in one hand and scoop out the flesh with a spoon, leaving 1/4-inch shell. Mix potato flesh with vegetable-cheese mixture. Add lemon juice, peas, salt, and pepper.

Set oven temperature at 350°F. Coat a vegetable dish with vegetable-oil cooking spray. Stuff potato shells with filling. Place potatoes in prepared dish, cover with aluminum foil, and bake for 15 to 20 minutes, or until thoroughly heated.

NOTE: IF YOU ARE STUFFING CHILLED PREVIOUSLY BAKED POTATOES, THEY MAY NEED AN EXTRA 5 TO 10 MINUTES IN THE OVEN TO HEAT THROUGH.

SACRED CHOW
522 Hudson Street
New York, New York 10014
212-337-0863

OPEN DAILY 7 A.M. TO 11 P.M.

Credit cards: AE, D, MC, V
Price: Moderate
Wheelchair accessible
No smoking
No alcohol

This hole-in-the-wall Greenwich Village natural foods cafe has only a few tables and a counter, but if you're seeking a cozy country-store feeling in the heart of the Big Apple, you'll find it at Sacred Chow.

Located in Manhattan's West Village, just a few blocks from the Hudson River, this charming spot also serves take-out food.

Cliff Prefer, co-owner and chef, explains that he opened his cafe because he was "unable to find a place to eat where the food was both delicious and free of animal products, sugar, wheat, and gluten."

This is, indeed, an animal-friendly place, and a statement on each menu lets the guests know all about it: "Sacred Chow's commitment to the earth, to nonviolence toward all forms of life, brings you unique, primarily organic specialty foods prepared without the use of any animal products. . . . Sacred Chow is devoted to providing a beautiful, innovative, and gentle food source that supports all life, human health, and our planet."

This clean, busy, and well-lighted restaurant has an open kitchen. Newspapers and magazines are available for reading, and people-watching is at its best from the counter that overlooks street traffic. A couple of chairs are on the sidewalk outside, and an elm tree offers shade.

The walls of Sacred Chow are reserved for displays of art. The crowd that patronizes the restaurant is a mix of local residents and guests who choose Sacred Chow because they suffer from allergies to specific foods.

Sacred Chow does a huge take-out business, and provides a weekly menu of take-out meals for those customers who want healthy, low-cholesterol, low-fat meals.

The staff is friendly, and if you have any questions about the food, don't hesitate to ask.

For breakfast, try one of the delicious Mixed-Fruit Muffins (fat- and wheat-free), Oatmeal Scones, or Vanilla Cream Danish Rolls. Lunch includes foods like Focaccia Pizza and freshly made soups and stews. Among the most popular entrées and salads are Grilled Marinated Tofu, Roasted Shiitake Risotto, and Eggplant-Spinach Moussaka.

Delicious pastries are available for dessert, such as the popular Almond Milk Chocolate Caramel Torte and Apple-Banana Pie. Delicious liquid treats include Cranberry Pear with Echinacea and Kiwi Dreams with Blue-Green Algae.

Fruited Couscous Cakes

Makes 5 cakes

Owner Cliff Prefer selected the Fruited Couscous Cakes because they are "quick and easy to make and contain no fat. Any fruit can be substituted for the peaches."

$1^1/2$ cups water
$1^1/2$ cups apple juice
$1^1/2$ cups couscous

$1/3$ cup orange blossom honey
Pinch of sea salt
$1^1/2$ teaspoons vanilla
$2/3$ cup raisins
2 peaches, peeled, pitted, and chopped

In a large saucepan, combine all ingredients except peaches and bring to boil. Reduce heat to low and stir constantly until all liquid is absorbed. Remove from heat. Fold peaches into couscous mixture.

Rinse muffin cups with hot water but do not dry. Fill 5 muffin cups three-fourths full with couscous mixture. Refrigerate for at least $1^1/2$ hours. Turn upside down and tap cup bottoms to unmold.

SPRING STREET NATURAL RESTAURANT
62 Spring Street
New York, New York 10012
212-966-0290

Price: Moderate
Credit cards: AE, DC, MC, V
Wheelchair accessible except for bathrooms
Smoking: In a special section
Alcohol: Beer and organic wines

One of the Big Apple's trendiest vegetarian restaurants, Spring Street Natural is located in the city's fashionable SoHo section. It's a colorful, vibrant neighborhood overflowing with chic galleries and hip boutiques, where this eatery strategically occupies a busy corner location not far from Little Italy and Chinatown.

The casual atmosphere is enhanced by slowly revolving fans, lots of plants, and dark wood floors. Expansive floor-to-ceiling windows front the large, airy two-level dining room, and the walls are painted a ruby color.

A long mahogany bar in one corner of the restaurant features a nice selection of organic wines. Both the restaurant and bar are popular with local artists, neighborhood residents, models, office workers, students, nearby shop owners, and tourists.

The menu is "chock-full of inventive vegetarian dishes," says co-owner Robert Schoen-holt. He adds that the entrées offered are different every day, and made mostly from organically grown ingredients. "The many fresh fish and seafood dishes use both line-caught and farm-fed fish. The poultry used is free range."

A popular dish is the Moroccan Vegetable Tagine (a Moroccan stew). Other menu favorites include Plantain-Crusted Florida Mahimahi (served with avocado, tomato and corn salsa, arroz moro, and snow peas), and Semolina Rigatoni (with herb-stewed tomatoes, pan-roasted garlic, and Moroccan cured olives sprinkled with shredded Asiago cheese).

Other favorites include Organic Potato Gnocchi (with vine-ripened tomatoes, grilled portobello mushrooms, pan-roasted garlic, fresh basil, and Gorgonzola), Pumpkin Ravioli (with huitlacoche and glazed shallots), and for breakfast mavens, the ever-popular Scrambled Tofu (with sweet onions, shiitakes, and fresh thyme).

Baked Saffron Polenta

Serves 6 as a main course

"One of the most popular specials on the menu is also a good example of the global concept of cooking here," explains co-owner Robert Schoenholt. "The Baked Saffron Polenta was created by chef Victor Hugo Sansberro.

"Polenta is not only a very popular dish in Italy, but also in South American countries. I'd suggest that this dish be accompanied with Stewed Green Lentils, another recipe created by our chef."

5 cups water
1 tablespoon olive oil
Salt to taste
1/2 teaspoon ground pepper

1 teaspoon ground nutmeg

Saffron to taste

1 pound instant polenta

1 cup (8 ounces) grated Parmesan cheese

12 slices Brie or Gorgonzola cheese (optional)

In a medium, heavy saucepan, bring water to a boil. Add oil, salt, pepper, nutmeg, and saffron.

Reduce heat to low. Gradually pour in polenta, stirring constantly with a wooden spoon.

Simmer for about 10 minutes, stirring frequently to avoid lumps. Add Parmesan cheese one ounce at a time, stirring until melted evenly into mix.

Cook for 5 minutes. Pour polenta into an oiled loaf pan.

Let cool completely. To serve, preheat oven to 350°F. Cut polenta into $1/2$-inch slices and place on a baking sheet. Bake until warm, about 10 minutes. Serve with Stewed Green Lentils recipe as a delicious main course. A tasty variation is to add sliced bread and crumbled gorgonzola to the polenta at the last minute of warming.

Stewed Green Lentils

Serves 6 as a side dish

5 cups water

1 cup dried French green lentils

1 tablespoon olive oil

1 tablespoon minced garlic

$1/2$ red bell pepper, seeded, deribbed, and diced
$1/2$ green bell pepper, seeded, deribbed, and diced
1 small red onion, diced
1 small leek, diced
1 tomato, chopped
Minced fresh basil and rosemary, to taste
Salt and ground pepper, to taste

In a medium saucepan, bring water to a boil. Add lentils, reduce heat, cover, and simmer until al dente, about 20 minutes. Drain and reserve liquid.

In a heavy, medium saucepan over low heat, heat olive oil and cook garlic for 2 or 3 minutes. Add peppers, onion, and leek and cook for about 5 minutes.

Add tomato, and cook another 5 minutes.

Add lentils and a little cooking liquid from lentils if necessary to make a soupy mixture.

Add basil, rosemary, salt, and pepper.

VILLAGE NATURAL HEALTH FOOD RESTAURANT
46 Greenwich Avenue
New York, New York 10011
212-727-0968

OPEN MONDAY THROUGH THURSDAY 11 A.M. TO 11 P.M., FRIDAY UNTIL MIDNIGHT; SATURDAY 9 A.M. TO MID-NIGHT, SUNDAY TO 10 P.M.; BRUNCHES SERVED SATURDAY AND SUNDAY 9 A.M. TO 4:30 P.M.

Price: Moderate
Credit cards: AE, D, MC, V
No wheelchair access
No smoking
Alcohol: Organic beer

In the heart of bustling Greenwich Village, located next to a bookstore that specializes in mystery novels, is one of the city's most popular natural foods eateries: the Village Natural Health Food Restaurant.

With its brick-trimmed walls, blonde wood decor, plentiful plants, and a working fireplace, this restaurant offers a casual, intimate, and restful dining environment with food that has won critical praise.

A few steps down from street level, the restaurant is filled with local residents, writers, mystery-novel aficionados, and area businessmen, all of whom enjoy the comfortable, homey ambiance and unhurried but excellent service.

A well-rounded and extensive menu with an Asian influence is featured here. Most of the food is organically raised, including the vegetables, vegetable proteins, grains, and beans.

Signature dishes include the popular Salmon Teriyaki, Spaghetti and Wheatballs (patties made from a delicious blend of wheat and vegetables lightly fried and served with steamed broccoli, artichoke noodles, tomato sauce, and garlic bread), and Oriental Vegetables with Udon (stir-fried veggies with tofu and udon noodles topped with nori).

There are plenty of salad choices, from a small side salad to main-dish salads, such as Green Salad with Salmon Roll (nori-rolled steamed salmon, broccoli, kale, and brown rice served on a bed of romaine, watercress, and spinach garnished with celery, broccoli, and cucumber). All dressings here are house-made and dairy-free.

All soups are nondairy and oil-free, including the special soup of the day. A soup that is always available and always excellent is the tasty miso.

If desserts are your thing, try the Wheat-Free Tofu-Blueberry Pie, the Tofu-Banana "Cream" Crumb, the Mocha Tofu Pie, or the Carrot Apple Walnut Cake with Tofu Frosting. Beer drinkers will enjoy the organic brew served here.

Tofu-Garlic-Dill Dressing

Makes 1 cup

Owner Lai Quach waxes enthusiastic about Village Natural's Tofu-Garlic-Dill Dressing. "This is a low-fat but creamy-tasting dressing made without dairy products. I watch the way my customers use it with their salads, and they look like they're ready to lick the container that it is served in. We serve lots of it."

1 cup silken tofu
8 garlic cloves
1 tablespoon minced fresh dill or 1 teaspoon dried dill

$1/4$ teaspoon sea salt
$1/4$ cup fresh lemon juice
$1/4$ cup red wine vinegar
$1/4$ cup vegetable oil (optional)

In a blender, combine all ingredients and puree until smooth. Store in an airtight container for up to 3 days.

Fresh-Apple Oatmeal

Serves 2

"The Fresh-Apple Oatmeal is another winner," Quach states. He adds that it's both a winter- and summertime best-seller. "It's simple to make at home and is fat-free and sugar-free. It's a delicious and healthy way to start your day, and lots of people who live and work around here do exactly that."

1 cup organic rolled oats
4 cups apple juice
$1/2$ teaspoon ground cinnamon
$1/4$ teaspoon ground nutmeg
Pinch of sea salt
1 teaspoon vanilla extract
Fresh or dried apple slices for garnish

In a large saucepan, combine all ingredients except apples and bring to a boil. Reduce heat, cover, and simmer for 15 minutes. Serve hot.

WHOLE-IN-THE-WALL
43 South Washington Street
Binghamton, New York 13903
607-722-0006

OPEN TUESDAY THROUGH SATURDAY 11:30 P.M. TO 9 P.M.

Price: Moderate
Credit cards: MC, V
Wheelchair access
No smoking
Alcohol: BYO

Situated in a fully restored 100-year-old building, this Binghamton storefront is one of a kind. The restoration began in 1978, when owner Eliot Fiks purchased the storefront. For three years he lovingly worked to restore the old structure, using wood recycled from demolished local houses including the Rose Mansion, once one of the most famous houses in town.

The renovation included removing layers of tile from the floors to reveal beautiful hardwood beneath. Wainscoting, handmade oak tables, and antique fixtures give Whole-in-the-Wall an old-fashioned, down-home feel. The eleven-table restaurant has been described by one writer as "warm and charming and giving off a feeling of old Binghamton."

Original artwork by dishwasher Bill Woolleet and waiter John Reed adorns the walls, and live piano music is featured each Friday and Saturday lunch and dinner. At Whole-in-the-Wall, you never know what musician might wander in for a bite to eat. Over the years, Bob Dylan, Kenny G., and other famous names in the music business have dropped by while on tour in the area.

According to Fiks, the restaurant's mission is to "serve the highest quality all-natural food in our own unique and sometimes offbeat way." And for more than 18 years he has been meeting that goal. "We've survived in the provinces because we prepare each meal with individual attention and have earned a loyal following," Fiks declares.

The extensive menu offers everything from appetizers to desserts, and whenever possible, organic products are used. Try the Creamy Mushroom Soup — a huge favorite that doesn't skimp on chunks of fresh mushrooms — or the Bapappetizer (homemade, thick baba ghanouj, with whole-wheat pita wedges).

Best-selling entrées include Stir-Fried Vegetables (your choice of tofu, tempeh, chicken, shrimp, or scallops); Hot and Spicy Vegetarian Chili; Mideast Platter (deep-fried exotically spiced falafel balls, salad, and baba ghanouj served with yogurt-sesame dressing and pita bread); Tempura (of all kinds); and Pesto Pie (pesto of the day, mozzarella, and sliced locally grown tomatoes).

Whole-in-the-Wall's pesto has been "discovered," and five varieties of it are now shipped throughout the Northeast to gourmet, natural foods stores, and directly to consumers. No alcohol is served on the premises, but you can bring your own alcoholic beverage of choice.

Sun-Dried Tomato Hummus

Makes about 2 cups

Fiks's choice for the restaurant's most popular dish is Sun-Dried Tomato Hummus. "The recipe was perfected by our head cook, Ethan. We think it can't be beat. It's all natural, high in protein and vitamins, and it tastes great! The hummus sticks to your ribs, but it's neither heavy nor rich."

1 cup dried chickpeas
1 small onion
1 small garlic clove
$1/4$ cup water
$1/4$ cup fresh lemon juice
$1/4$ cup olive oil
$1/4$ cup tahini
$1^1/2$ teaspoons salt
$1/2$ teaspoon ground pepper
$1/2$ teaspoon garlic powder
$3/4$ teaspoon Asian sesame oil
2 tablespoons thinly sliced oil-packed sun-dried tomatoes
$1/4$ cup finely chopped green onions

Rinse and pick over the chickpeas. Soak in water to cover overnight. Drain. In a soup pot, combine chickpeas with water to cover by 2 inches. Bring to a boil, reduce heat, cover, and simmer until tender, $2^1/2$ to 3 hours. Drain.

In a blender or food processor, combine onion, garlic, and water and puree until smooth. Add all remaining ingredients except sun-dried tomatoes and green onions and process until smooth. Transfer to a bowl and mix in green onions and tomatoes.

ZEN PALATE
34 Union Square East
New York, New York 10003
212-614-9291

663 Ninth Avenue
New York, New York 10036
212-582-1669

2170 Broadway
New York, New York 10024
212-501-7768

OPEN DAILY 11:30 A.M. TO 10:45 P.M. (HOURS OF OTHER BRANCHES VARY SLIGHTLY)

Price: Cafe inexpensive; dining room moderate
Credit cards: AE, MC, V
Wheelchair accessible except for bathroom
No smoking
Alcohol: BYO

At Zen Palate's popular flagship restaurant on Union Square East, directly across the street from historic Union Square Park, the ambiance is one of peacefulness and restfulness. This is elegant, upscale gourmet vegetarian dining at its best.

The street-level cafe is more casual than the upstairs dining area, but the food is no less delicious or lovingly prepared. In the cafe, guests can sit at the counter or at tables surrounding it. Part of the fun of dining in the cafe is watching the chefs bustle about in the open kitchen.

The upstairs dining room is a different world: a peaceful atmosphere, formally dressed waiters, and tables covered with white tablecloths.

Although the menus at both locations are similar, the food served in the dining room is more expensive. Popular dishes include Hot and Sour Vegetable Soup, Tasty Morsels (which includes everything from Taro Spring Rolls and Steamed Vegetable Dumplings to the Zen Vegi-Burger, made with sunflower seeds, kale, and brown rice).

Excellent pasta dishes are found on the menu (try the Spinach Linguine Salad with Sesame Peanut Dressing). Other best-sellers include Curry Supreme (tender soy protein with potatoes and carrots in a mild curry sauce, served with a taro spring roll and brown rice) and Sautéed Artichoke with Basil (artichoke, tomato, and soy protein in black bean sauce seasoned with basil, taro spring roll, and brown rice).

Another very popular dish is Shepherd's Pie Croquets (minced vegetables surrounded by mashed potatoes, a basil moo-shu roll, and pickled cabbage). Almost every dish features organically raised products when they are available, and all are low in cholesterol.

For a unique liquid treat, try the refreshing Rice Milk Shake and Soy Bean Milk. Freshly squeezed juices are also available, along with an interesting array of teas, ranging from pineapple to cranberry.

Dessert-lovers will enjoy the Banana Pie (banana with nondairy yogurt, and shredded almonds), the Pear Pie, and the Tofu Honey Pie.

Curry Supreme

Serves 2 as a main course

General manager Charley Chaung says of the Curry Supreme: "It's one of our customers' favorite dishes, and because it's not difficult to make you can sample the kind of food we prepare right in your own home. Then, maybe, after being impressed, you'll make a reservation so that you can taste our other menu delights."

4 ounces soy protein, cut into cubes

1 tablespoon soy sauce

1 tablespoon grated fresh ginger

2 teaspoons molasses or packed brown sugar

1 tablespoon cooking wine

1/4 teaspoon ketchup

Soy bean oil for deep-frying, plus 1 tablespoon

1 to 2 unpeeled potatoes, cut into cubes

3 carrots, cut into cubes

1/2 white onion, finely chopped

1 tablespoon curry powder

Soak soy protein in warm water for 3 hours. Then gently squeeze out about half the water (don't make it too dry).

In a small bowl, combine soy sauce, ginger, and molasses or brown sugar and add wine. Dilute this mixture with equal amount of water. Mix in ketchup. Soak soy protein in this sauce for 1 hour. Drain.

Pour oil into a large, heavy skillet to a depth of 2 inches. Heat oil until it smokes. Turn off heat and add soy protein. Cook 1 minute, then remove soy from pan.

Heat oil again and fry potatoes until light golden. Remove from pan.

Cook carrots in boiling water to cover until al dente. Drain, reserving water.

In a large, heavy saucepan over medium heat, heat 1 tablespoon oil and sauté onion until golden. Add curry powder, stir, and turn off heat. Stir in reserved water from carrots. Mix in potatoes, carrots, and soy protein. Add water to cover. Bring to a boil, reduce heat, and simmer for approximately 45 minutes. Taste and adjust seasoning.

ANOTHERTHYME
109 North Gregson Street
Durham, North Carolina 27701
919-682-5225

OPEN FOR LUNCH TUESDAY THROUGH FRIDAY 11:30 A.M. TO 2 P.M.; DINNER SUNDAY THROUGH THURSDAY 5:30 P.M. TO 9:30 P.M., FRIDAY AND SATURDAY TO 10:30 P.M.

Price: Moderate to expensive
Credit cards: AE, MC, V
Wheelchair accessible
Smoking: At bar only
Alcohol: Full service bar

Anotherthyme, which opened its doors in 1982, is a local landmark in Durham. Following in the footsteps of its predecessor, Somethyme, an all-vegetarian eatery, this popular restaurant has developed a reputation for exquisite natural foods cuisine.

Anotherthyme's owner and executive chef, Mary Bacon, likes to say that her establishment not only provides nourishment for the body, but is an active community partner as well.

"We're a warm, broadly appealing community center for a diverse and always interesting group of locals and the community surrounding Duke University," she states.

Although Anotherthyme is no longer strictly vegetarian, Bacon emphasizes that the restaurant's nonmeat dishes prove that "dishes based on vegetables and seafood can match, as well as surpass, their meatier cousins."

Anotherthyme has a relaxed and casual atmosphere. Tables are situated to allow patrons to enjoy intimate conversation, and no one is ever rushed to finish a meal. "Turning over tables at a fast pace is not a priority," asserts Bacon.

The restaurant's interior is bathed in soft light. And Bacon's artistic ability — which equals her culinary skills in the kitchen — is in evidence in the painted brick exterior and the faux-finished interior. Original contemporary artworks complement the enticing aromas and flavors of the food.

The restaurant has a cozy and friendly bar, which, in addition to the full service bar, offers a wine list with more than 100 well-chosen selections, as well as a broad by-the-glass program.

The extensive menu features innovative cuisine from around the world, as well as traditional regional American favorites; organic ingredients are used when available. You may wish to begin your culinary adventure with Thai Shrimp Soup (snow peas, straw mushrooms, tofu, and red peppers in a lemongrass seafood broth).

A popular Southwestern American entrée is the Mushroom Poblano Burrito (sautéed portobello, shiitake, and domestic mushrooms, onions, and poblano chilies in a soft tortilla, served with salsa verde, black beans, and fresh goat cheese).

Linguine with White Clam Sauce (house-made linguine with a spicy white herb sauce, garnished with North Carolina littleneck clams) is a favorite, as is the Greek Chicken (grilled herbed chicken breast layered with tomatoes, fresh goat cheese, and sun-dried tomatoes, served on garlicky-buttered pita bread).

For nonvegetarians, a popular dish is Fried Chicken Yukon Gold (a chicken breast rolled in fresh herbs, bread crumbs, almonds, and Parmesan cheese, then fried and served with mashed potatoes and steamed broccoli). If you still have room, Anotherthyme offers a mouthwatering selection of desserts, espresso drinks, and after-dinner drinks.

Greek Pasta

Serves 4 as a main course

"Greek Pasta is an international favorite at the restaurant," says Mary Bacon. "It proves our philosophy that the flavor of seafood and vegetables can surpass the taste of meat."

SAUCE

1/4 cup butter

1/4 cup olive oil

1/4 cup minced garlic

3 cups medium shrimp

4 tablespoons capers, chopped (plus juice)

4 tablespoons Greek olives, pitted and sliced

6 tablespoons chopped roasted red peppers

4 tablespoons basil pesto

Pinch of ground pepper

1 tablespoon minced fresh thyme leaves

6 tablespoons fresh lemon juice

1 1/3 cup vegetable stock

6 cups fettuccine

3/4 cup crumbled feta cheese

1 teaspoon minced fresh oregano, plus 1 sprig oregano for garnish

Lemon wedges for garnish

To make sauce: In a large skillet, melt butter with olive oil over medium heat. Add garlic and sauté until golden. Add shrimp and sauté until just pink, 2 to 3 minutes. Add all remaining sauce ingredients and stir well. Set aside and keep warm.

In a large pot of salted boiling water, cook pasta until al dente, 2 to 3 minutes. Drain. Add pasta to pan with warm sauce, toss to coat, and cook over low heat for 1 1/2 minutes.

Put in a warm pasta serving bowl and top with feta cheese and oregano. Garnish with oregano sprig and lemon wedges.

MUSTARD SEED MARKET CAFE
3885 West Market Street
Akron, Ohio 44333
330 666-7333

OPEN MONDAY THROUGH THURSDAY 11 A.M. TO 8 P.M., SATURDAY TO 9 P.M., AND SUNDAY TO 5 P.M.

Price: Moderate
Credit cards: MC, V
Wheelchair accessible
No smoking
Alcohol: Beer and wine

Located on the mezzanine of one of the largest natural foods stores in the Midwest, this cafe has been described by guests as an "unexpected jewel," according to cafe manager Barbara Schenk.

While the scene below is one of hustle and bustle, upstairs is a tranquil world of soft carpeting, linen napkins, and tasteful artwork.

Skylights above the espresso and juice bars provide plenty of natural light for the plants found throughout the cafe, and live music is featured Thursday through Sunday.

The Mustard Seed's menu emphasizes vegetarian dishes, including macrobiotic and vegan meals, but seafood, poultry, and some meat entrées are also offered.

A popular starter is the Vegetarian Nori Make (sweet brown rice seasoned with ube plum — a variety originally cultivated in Japan — and tahini, wrapped in nori, stuffed with organic carrots, cabbage, cucumbers, and green onions, and served with real wasabi and pickled ginger).

A luncheon sandwich that draws lots of attention is the Tempeh Reuben (seasoned tempeh served on sourdough rye with Thousand Island dressing, organic sauerkraut, and Emmentaler cheese).

The dinner menu features everything from Chicken Stir-Fry to Whole Foods Cuisine (a complete macrobiotic meal of miso soup, grain, greens, vegetable, protein, and a nondairy cookie for dessert).

The restaurant also offers specials that are as varied as they are creative. Favorites include Nut-Encrusted Skate (ocean skate encrusted with pecans, panfried, and served with mushrooms and spring garlic). Also popular is the Vegan Meatless Loaf (made with tofu, oats, and seasonings, and served with shiitake mushroom gravy, organic brown rice, and steamed vegetables).

On Sundays, the cafe serves up a breakfast buffet with fresh fruit, muffins, hot entrées, and omelets made to order.

Tempeh Piccata

Serves 4 as a main course

Chef Dan Remark says, "One of the fun aspects of cooking in the natural foods scene is introducing new food combinations to those who are more traditional in their eating styles. The Tempeh Piccata is a familiar classic, but tempeh is used instead of meat and miso in place of butter."

4 tempeh cutlets or burgers, cut in half horizontally
1/4 cup whole-wheat flour

1 cup fresh lemon juice

1 cup dry white wine

$1/2$ cup white miso

2 teaspoon minced garlic

1 tablespoon capers, drained

8 ounces dried mushroom linguini

$1/4$ teaspoon minced fresh thyme

1 tablespoon minced fresh parsley

$1/2$ teaspoon minced fresh chives

Preheat oven to 350°F. Dredge cutlets or burgers in flour. In a small bowl, combine lemon juice, wine, miso, garlic, and capers. In a large oven-proof skillet over medium-high heat, heat oil. Add tempeh and brown on both sides. Cover and bake for 10 minutes.

Meanwhile, in a large pot of salted boiling water, cook linguine until al dente. Drain.

Add miso mixture to tempeh and bring to a boil. Serve over linguini and top with herbs.

Bulgur Waldorf

Serves 2 to 4 as a side dish

"I chose this recipe for the simple reason that it is our all-time favorite," says Dan. "It's a vegan twist on the Waldorf Salad, which is also very popular on the menu."

3 cups apple juice

$1^1/4$ cups packed raisins

2 cups bulgur wheat

$1/2$ cup maple syrup

$1/4$ cup fresh lemon juice

$1/2$ teaspoon vanilla extract

1 cup walnuts, toasted and chopped

3 large apples, peeled, cored, and cut into $1/2$-inch dice

In a large saucepan, combine $2^1/2$ cups apple juice and raisins. Bring to a boil. Turn off heat. Stir in bulgur, cover, and set aside.

Combine maple syrup, lemon juice, vanilla, and remaining $1/2$ cup apple juice. Add walnuts and apples and blend.

THE COLUMBIAN CAFE
1114 Marine Drive
Astoria, Oregon 97103
503-325-2233

OPEN FOR BREAKFAST AND LUNCH MONDAY THROUGH FRIDAY 8 A.M. TO 2 P.M.; BRUNCH SATURDAY 10 A.M. TO 2 P.M.; DINNER WEDNESDAY THROUGH SATURDAY 5 TO 9 P.M.; BRUNCH SUNDAY 9 A.M. TO 4 P.M.

Price: Moderate to expensive
No credit cards
Wheelchair accessible
No smoking
Alcohol: Full bar

Visitors who spot the painted red coffee cups above the red and white awning that shelters tables outside the Columbian Cafe are instantly transported back to the 1930s when the cafe was a five-cent burger shop. But that old-fashioned look is also sometimes the cause of a bit of confusion.

Owner and chef Uriah Hulsey chuckles that people who have read glowing reviews about the fare served here "often walk right by the cafe, mistaking it for a dive rather than the gourmet vegetarian restaurant they were seeking."

Once inside the cafe, however, guests are instantly charmed not only by the old-fashioned and intimate ambiance, but by the tantalizing aroma of the made-from-scratch food being prepared.

The cafe is decorated with pepper-shaped lights and dried-pepper and garlic braids. A collection of old juicers and 1950s porcelain fruits add to the decor.

The old diner-style counter seats nine and looks like one James Dean might have enjoyed sitting at before taking off on his motorcycle. Besides the counter and three booths, annex seating for 30 or more has been added.

Best of all is the tantalizing aroma of vegetarian dishes being cooked right behind that counter. "It's the smell of the cafe that captures people and makes them fall in love with it," boasts Hulsey.

If you like reading while you eat, then check out the rear of the cafe where a cedar shelf contains a library of diverse magazines.

Among the popular dishes served here are Chef's Mercy and Seafood Mercy, named so, according to Hulsey, because "you may name your preferred cooking spice temperature, and all the rest is at the chef's mercy." Crepes are a specialty, and range from mushroom and broccoli to cheese.

Be prepared for a bit of a wait. "Every dish is its own creation," Hulsey states. "Everything is prepared individually. The food is always worth the wait."

Sturgeon Piccata

Serves one as a main course

Waiter Marco Davis says the restaurant began serving Sturgeon Piccata in early summer 1996. "The smells this dinner creates as it is being prepared are unlike any I have ever known. For weeks I suffered under its intoxicating scent. Often I found my toes curled as I was waiting tables; the dinner was calling my name, begging me to savor its essence.

"I arranged to have a night off so that I could enjoy it fully. I started my meal with a wilted spinach salad (steamed on the grill with tomatoes, garlic, onions, blue cheese, and walnuts). Amazing!

"I then teased myself with a glass of Stags Leap Petite Syrah 1991. The romance of the dish began — the smells of the butter, the snap of the sturgeon as it was laid in the pan, the ding of the timer as the pasta was finished cooking — my Sturgeon Picatta arrived.

"My oh my — every bite was like butter in my mouth! I will never forget that night or resist sharing it with all those I know."

3 to 4 slices of sturgeon
Italian bread crumbs for coating
1 tablespoon butter
20 capers, drained
$1/4$ cup dry white wine
Squeeze of lemon juice
5 sun-dried tomatoes, cut into julienne
Hot pasta of choice

Lightly coat the sturgeon with crumbs. In a large skillet, melt butter over medium heat and add capers. When capers open, add sturgeon. Add wine and lemon juice and flash-fry (2 to 3 minutes) sturgeon over medium heat.

Turn sturgeon over and add sun-dried tomatoes. Cook sturgeon for another 2 to 3 minutes. Serve over pasta.

PLAINFIELD'S MAYUR: CUISINE OF INDIA
852 SW 21st Street
Portland, Oregon 97205-1620
503-223-2995

OPEN DAILY 5:30 TO 10 P.M.

Price: Expensive
All major credit cards
Wheelchair accessible
Smoking: In limited sections
Alcohol: An award-winning wine list
with more than 200 selections

Located in a large Victorian historic mansion built at the turn of the century, this elegant dining establishment featuring the cuisine of India offers not only excellent vegetarian meals but is an Indian art gallery as well.

Dining here is like eating at the table of some fabled Indian rajah. The formal dining room is filled with high-backed chairs and tables covered with white tablecloths. The table settings feature fine European crystal and china. Full silver service is also part of the elegant setting.

Other dining areas are located throughout this landmark home, from an upstairs dining room perfect for private parties or business meetings to an outdoor patio that is open during the summer months.

But Plainfield's Mayur offers more than just great dining. This award-winning eatery also hosts a gallery filled with artworks from some of India's finest artists. Guests are invited to tour the gallery before or after their meals, or to wander through the palace-like dining areas, where more art can be viewed.

Owners Rich and Rekha Plainfield explain that "our goal is to serve you in elegant surroundings while still preserving casual ambiance. So sit back, relax, and let us treat you to the royal Indian tradition of hospitality."

The dining room features a unique tandoori open kitchen, the only one of its kind in the state. While you wait for your meal, you can watch the chefs cooking their famous tandoori breads and other dishes in large clay tandoors, ovens whose temperatures can go up to 1,000 degrees.

The chefs at Plainfield's Mayur — Sanskrit for peacock (the national bird of India), believe that the secret to the exotic flavors of Indian cuisine are the masalas, blends of individually roasted and ground spices. All of the masalas used here are family recipes that have been handed down from generation to generation.

Plainfield's Mayur, which first opened in 1977 in northwest Portland before moving to its current location in 1986, also hosts special dining events. One of the most popular is the Tuesday night traditional Indian Ayurvedic meal. Ayurvedic means "the knowledge of life," and this meal is designed to promote health based on an ancient system adopted from India's books of wisdom.

A popular offering on the menu is the Dahi Wada, an appetizer made of crispy fried lentil balls in a slightly spicy ginger, coriander, and yogurt sauce. Also popular is the Tomato Coconut Soup, a delicious combination of tomato, coconut, fried curry leaves, and spices, garnished with fresh coriander.

The hearty Biryani — another best-seller — is a dish normally reserved for special occasions in India (basmati rice baked in a mixture of saffron, vegetables, spices, and either prawns, lamb, chicken, or paneer — a mild cheese made with cow's milk — and garnished with nuts, coconut, and coriander leaves and silver leaf). Also favored is the Shahi Subji Korma (carrots, potatoes, turnips, peas, and paneer braised in an ivory white almond-yogurt sauce).

Wine goes perfectly with these specials, and you can choose from 200 selections on the restaurant's award-winning wine list. For dessert, try the yogurt pudding; it's simply scrumptious.

Shrikhanda (Yogurt Pudding)

Serves 4 as a dessert

Rich and Rehka point to the Shrikhanda, or yogurt pudding, as one of the restaurant's all-time favorites. "This dessert is served on very special occasions in India, and it's a favorite here as well. So don't miss trying this one. Even though it is very simple to make, it is coveted for its smooth creamy texture and sweet tangy taste. Make sure that you pick a good-quality yogurt with live cultures and no thickeners or stabilizers."

1 quart plain natural yogurt
$1/4$ teaspoon saffron grind and soak in $1/8$ teaspoon hot water
$1/4$ teaspoon ground nutmeg
$1/2$ to 1 cup sugar
Sliced almonds for garnish

Line a large sieve with 2 layers of cheesecloth and place sieve over a bowl. Empty yogurt into sieve and let sit at room temperature overnight to drain. Transfer yogurt to a medium bowl and add saffron mixture, nutmeg, and sugar to taste, depending on the sourness of the yogurt. Spoon into small custard cups and garnish with sliced almonds.

CHERRY STREET CHINESE VEGETARIAN RESTAURANT
1010 Cherry Street
Philadelphia, Pennsylvania 19107
215-923-3663

OPEN MONDAY THROUGH THURSDAY 11:30 A.M. TO 10 P.M., FRIDAY AND SATURDAY UNTIL 11 P.M.; SUNDAY 12:30 TO 10 P.M.

Price: Moderate
All major credit cards except DC
Wheelchair accessible
No smoking
Alcohol: BYO

Located in the heart of Philadelphia's Chinatown, this bustling and popular restaurant not only offers a wide selection of vegan and macrobiotic options, but the food served here is kosher as well.

The 180-seat restaurant is on the beaten track for tourists visiting the City of Brotherly Love's Chinatown, students from the University of Pennsylvania, and members of the city's Jewish population with a yen for pork-free Chinese food.

Cherry Street Chinese Vegetarian Restaurant is an attractive, luxurious bi-level restaurant. Its walls are covered with beautiful watercolors from mainland China, and there are comfortable armchairs at each of the establishment's linen-covered tables.

The interior walls are beige, with natural wood trim, while the copper floors are painted gray and blue. Flowers are in evidence everywhere throughout the restaurant.

If you're dining with a boyfriend or girlfriend, you might be inspired to take your relationship a step further as wedding parties are a frequent event at this unique Chinese eatery.

The restaurant menu features everything from vegetable and tofu dishes to mock-meat meals. Among the favorites are Dynasty Chicken (mock chicken with a rich, delicious spicy brown sauce, cauliflower, and broccoli), Rainbow Bean Curd (steamed tofu, shiitake mushrooms, carrots, mock ham, and green kale), and the Gourmet Veggie Basket (oyster mushrooms, Chinese green kale, burdock, broccoli, snow peas, and fresh water chestnuts served in a taro root basket). Other specialties include Watercress and Tofu Soup and Eggplant in Black Bean Sauce.

Emerald Three-Mix Soup

Serves 2 to 4 as an appetizer

Owner Raymond Fung writes that the Emerald Three-Mix Soup is a favorite at his restaurant because of its color and fragrance. "I named it Emerald Three-Mix because of its green color, and because there are three main ingredients in the soup.

"The color is created by asparagus juice, which is expensive but I like the way it looks and the fragrance it creates when the soup is ready. Although I enjoy adding colors to food, all of our coloring is completely natural. Besides asparagus juice, at the restaurant we use carrot juice, spinach juice, and beet juice."

4 dried shiitake mushrooms
1/2 teaspoon of vegetable oil
4 asparagus stalks, cut diagonally
1 ounce enoki mushrooms, cut into 1-inch lengths

2 cups vegetable stock
2 cups asparagus juice (see note)
1 teaspoon salt
$^1/_2$ teaspoon sugar (optional)
$^1/_2$ teaspoon cornstarch mixed with water until creamy
$^1/_2$ teaspoon of Asian sesame oil (optional)
Pinch of white pepper

Soak mushrooms in hot water for 15 minutes. Drain and cut into strips.

In a large, heavy skillet over medium heat, heat vegetable oil and sauté shiitake mushrooms, asparagus, and enoki mushrooms for 5 minutes. Add vegetable stock. Bring to a boil and cook for 1 minute. Add asparagus juice. Bring to a boil again and add salt and optional sugar. Slowly pour in cornstarch mixture stirring until soup thickens. Add optional sesame oil and white pepper. Bring soup to a boil again. Serve.

NOTE: TO MAKE ASPARAGUS JUICE, BOIL ASPARAGUS IN WATER UNTIL TENDER. RESERVE WATER.

DOE'S PITA PLUS
334 East Bay Street
Charleston, South Carolina 29401
843-577-3179

651 Johnnie Dodds
Mt. Pleasant, South Carolina 29464
843-971-2080

5134 North Rhett
North Charleston, South Carolina 29405
843-745-0026

OPEN DAILY FROM 8 A.M. TO 8:30 P.M.

Price: Inexpensive
No credit cards
Wheelchair accessible
No smoking
No alcohol

Currently in its seventh year of operation, and now boasting three locations, this casual natural foods restaurant specializes in healthful low-fat and nonfat dishes, many of which have a Middle Eastern flavor.

It's an eatery favored by local businessmen, students, and "anyone concerned about their cholesterol count. Art-lovers will enjoy these establishments, which feature the work of local artists."

Ethnic-style dishes include Lebanese Potato Salad (with freshly cooked potatoes, scallions, parsley, olive oil, lemon juice, and garlic), Bulgur and Tuna Salad (bulgur wheat, tuna, Spanish onions, parsley, a splash of olive oil, and rice vinegar), and Cohar's Bean Salad — an Armenian favorite. Everything is made on the premises, and only the freshest organic ingredients are used when available. Doe's Pita Plus also makes its own fat-free pita bread, and like all the other dishes here, all the pocket sandwich fillings are made from scratch.

While the restaurant is known for its large variety of vegetarian items, it also caters to customers who relish chicken. A year-round favorite is the Chicken and Sun-Dried Plums (freshly cooked chicken breast, sun-dried plums, celery, and scallions mixed with nonfat yogurt, garnished with lettuce, tomatoes, and sprouts).

Among the Doe's Pita Plus most popular vegetarian dishes are the hummus, tabbouleh, baba ghanouj, and Lebanese Fatoosh (a small garden salad with pita chips and house dressing).

Food can be purchased for takeout by the pint or half-pint. There are also offerings to keep kids happy: a Pita Dog (turkey frank with garnishes of choice) and a Peanut Butter and Banana Sandwich Pita. Yum!

Curried Chicken Yogurt Salad

Serves 4 to 6 as a lunch course or sandwich

Owner Doe McGuinness notes that not only is the Curried Chicken Yogurt Salad a favorite among her customers, but "it also is used by many as a dip or spread. It is simple to make. It's also a good example of how we can make tasty food and at the same time reduce fat and cholesterol."

4 cups diced and cooked chicken breast meat
1 cup chopped celery
1 1/2 cups diced apples

1 teaspoon salt

$1/2$ teaspoon ground pepper

1 tablespoon curry powder

$1/2$ cup golden raisins

$1^1/2$ to 2 cups plain nonfat yogurt

In a large bowl, mix all ingredients together. Taste and adjust seasoning. Refrigerate overnight, then serve near room temperature.

SLICE OF LIFE RESTAURANT AND BAKERY
1811 Division Street
Nashville, Tennessee 37203
615-329-2525

OPEN MONDAY AND SUNDAY 7 A.M. TO 4 P.M., TUESDAY THROUGH THURSDAY TO 9 P.M., FRIDAY AND SATURDAY TO 10 P.M.

Price: Inexpensive to moderate
All major credit cards
No wheelchair access
No smoking
Alcohol: Small selection of wines

Located in the former home of the late country music star Marty Robbins, Slice of Life is a perfect place to take a breather as you two-step your way through Nashville's famous Music Row, located a couple of blocks away.

The singer's former home is a sprawling ranch house. Stained-glass windows and skylights provide plenty of light for the magnificent potted trees found throughout the restaurant, while the marble walls are a perfect backdrop for the large abstract paintings created by local Tennessee artists.

Slice of Life prides itself on serving healthy and delicious meals. All of its food is free of sugar and preservatives. Vegan and macrobiotic options are available.

One popular entrée is Tiger Food (brown rice, tofu, onions, peppers, and a nutritional yeast). Other favorite choices are the Bean Burrito, stuffed with sour cream and salsa, and Tofu-Spinach Lasagna.

Desserts are spectacular here, and the only sweeteners used are honey, fructose, or apple juice. A popular low-fat favorite is the Poppy Seed Cake.

Veggie Burger

Makes 4 to 6 burgers

$4^2/3$ cups rolled oats

$1^3/4$ cups textured vegetable protein (TVP)

1 small onion, finely chopped

4 eggs, beaten

1 ounce salt or Spike

$3/4$ cup nutritional yeast

2 cups water

$1/8$ teaspoon ground pepper

1 tablespoon tamari soy sauce

1 small zucchini, finely chopped

1 small summer squash, finely chopped

1 small carrot, finely chopped

In a large bowl, combine all ingredients and mix well.

In a large skillet, on medium high heat, cook formed burgers for about 5 minutes.

WILD OATS

1801 Union Avenue		5101 Sanderlin, Suite 124
Memphis, Tennessee 38104	*and*	Memphis, Tennessee 38117
901-725-4823		901-685-2293

DELI: OPEN MONDAY THROUGH FRIDAY 9 A.M. TO 9 P.M., SATURDAY TO 8 P.M.; SUNDAY 11 A.M. TO 6 P.M.

KITCHEN: OPEN MONDAY THROUGH SATURDAY 11 A.M. TO 7 P.M., SUNDAY TO 4 P.M.

Price: Inexpensive
Credit cards: AE, D, MC, V
Wheelchair accessible
No smoking
No alcohol

These two Wild Oats cafes feature lots of green plants and bold colors, and the convenience of being in the heart of a natural foods market.

At the Sanderlin location, the dining area is glass enclosed. Alas, the view is pure parking lot. The Union Avenue location, with its multi-level ceiling occasionally features live music.

The Wild Oats cafes offer nutritious and tasty food that is free of artificial flavors and coloring, preservatives or additives. Only dolphin-safe tuna and range-free chicken are served, and organic ingredients are used whenever possible.

Each day the cafes offer a vegetarian, low-fat, and seafood special. One of the best-selling salads is the delicious Cashew Noodle (spaghetti, green onions, and cashews tossed with a dressing made from toasted sesame oil, cashew butter, tamari, and red pepper flakes).

The cafes remain true to their southern roots by featuring Rice and Beans, along with a tasty Cajun Shrimp Salad. For breakfast, choose from a variety of muffins including blueberry, "magic" bran, apricot, and lemon poppy seed.

Tabbouleh

Serves 2 as a side dish

Manager Julie Ray says the Tabbouleh is a best-selling deli item. "It's nutritious, beautiful, and very tasty. It's a standard here, along with the hummus."

1 cup bulgur wheat
$1^1/4$ cups hot water
$1/4$ cup fresh lemon juice
$1/4$ cup extra-virgin olive oil
3 tablespoons minced fresh mint, or 1 tablespoon dried mint
1 tablespoon salt
1 tablespoon minced garlic
1 cup minced fresh parsley
8 green onions, finely chopped
1 large tomato, chopped
1 bell pepper, seeded, deribbed, and chopped

In a large bowl, combine bulgar, water, lemon juice, oil, mint, salt, and garlic. Mix well. Fold in parsley, green onions, tomato, and pepper. Let sit at room temperature for 2 hours.

Hummus

Makes 2 cups

2 cups dried chickpeas (garbanzo beans) or black beans
Small piece of kombu
$1/2$ bunch fresh parsley, stemmed and chopped
$1/2$ bunch green onions, chopped
$1/3$ cup fresh lemon juice
$1^1/2$ teaspoons salt
Cayenne pepper to taste
$1/4$ cup extra-virgin olive oil
$1/3$ cup tahini
$1^1/2$ teaspoons chopped garlic

Wash and pick over beans. Soak overnight in water to cover by 2 inches. Drain. In a soup pot, combine beans, kombu, and water to cover by 2 inches. Bring to a boil, reduce heat to a simmer, cover, and cook until tender, about 3 hours for chickpeas and $1^1/2$ hours for black beans.

Pour beans into a colander to drain. Rinse under cold running water until cool.

In a blender or food processor, combine beans (in batches, if necessary) with remaining ingredients and puree until smooth. Store in airtight container in refrigerator for up to 3 days. Serve with pita bread or chips.

KALACHANDJI'S RESTAURANT AND PALACE
5430 Gurley Avenue
Dallas, Texas 75223
214-821-1048

OPEN FOR LUNCH TUESDAY THROUGH FRIDAY 11:30 A.M. TO 2 P.M.; SATURDAY NOON TO 3 P.M., DINNER TUESDAY THROUGH SUNDAY 5:30 TO 9 P.M.

Price: Moderate
Credit cards: MC, V
Wheelchair accessible
No smoking
No alcohol

Kalachandji's Restaurant and Palace is a top-rated vegetarian restaurant located in a residential area of East Dallas. Indoor dining is supplemented with dining in one of the city's nicest courtyard patios. The focal points of the courtyard are a fountain and a tree surrounded by cascading plants.

During summer months, customers are cooled by fans that twirl above each table. Outdoor dining is possible even during chillier weather, thanks to heaters.

The restaurant's interior is tastefully done. Spanish-style stucco walls and red tile floors are accented with beautiful arched windows of brightly colored stained glass. Light strains of Indian music add to the relaxing atmosphere of this pleasant vegetarian eatery.

The main courses change daily, but there is always an ample salad bar and dessert favorites like kheer (sweet rice pudding made with milk and cream, with fruits, raisins, or toasted nuts mixed in). Barbecued Tofu and an excellent Vegetarian Quiche are also available on a rotating basis. Fresh house-made breads are served with every meal, and organic ingredients are used in food preparation. The restaurant prides itself on the fact that no preservatives are used here.

Other best-selling dishes include Halvah (farina cake pudding), Lentil Soup, and Pappadams (crispy, spicy wafers). Also popular are the Pakoras (deep-fried fruit or vegetable fritters).

If you enjoy tea, Tamarind Tea is a tasty brew that goes well with the Halvah. After dessert, you might want to check out the Indian gift shop.

Blueberry Halvah

Serves 4 as a dessert

According to the restaurant, "Halvah is a constant favorite at Kalachandji's Restaurant, and the Blueberry Halvah tops the list. Halvah is a rich fluffy dessert of sweetened farina combined with fruits and nuts, a delightful anytime treat.

"Halvah is a great dish that can be served chilled, or hot right from the stove. The following recipe can be made with raisins, nuts, or any fruit you like."

1 cup farina
1/2 cup (1 stick) butter
2 cups water
1 teaspoon vanilla extract
1/2 cup fresh or frozen blueberries
1 cup sugar

In a medium saucepan, melt butter over medium-low heat and sauté farina until it is golden brown and the consistency looks (and sounds) like coarse, wet sand. In another medium saucepan, bring water to a boil and add vanilla and blueberries. Return to a boil and immediately add farina. Stir in sugar and cook over low heat until mixture thickens. Pour into 4 serving dishes. Serve hot or chilled.

A MOVEABLE FEAST HEALTHFOOD STORE
AND NATURAL CAFE
2202 West Alabama Street
Houston, Texas 77798
713-528-3585

OPEN DAILY (EXCEPT HOLIDAYS) 11 A.M. TO 9 P.M.

Price: Inexpensive to moderate
Credit cards: AE, DC, MC, V
Wheelchair accessible
No smoking
No alcohol

If you're a Hemingway fan, you will instantly recognize the source of this establishment's name — the title of his autobiographical tribute to Paris. Like the Parisian cafes of its namesake, A Moveable Feast is a place where people gather to "celebrate life, socialize, and to freely discuss art, philosophy, and food."

Located in a red brick two-story building, this independent, family-owned neighborhood store and restaurant has been serving the community since 1971. Office manager Barbara Buckle states that "the emphasis has always been on the integrity of the product selection and personalized service."

The restaurant, which produces its own private-label food line, has a fresh, airy look to it. The bright L-shaped room is surrounded with large windows that look out on a nearby residential neighborhood, and everywhere there are hanging baskets filled with green ivy. Comic strips and pictures adorn the walls.

The restaurant is intended to showcase the foods sold in the store and, according to Buckle, "to demonstrate that healthy natural foods are also delicious and attractive — which has been the mission of this business since its founding."

You will find a diverse dining crowd here because not only is this one of the "best health food stores and natural foods restaurants in the state of Texas," according to one newspaper review, but A Moveable Feast is also a community resource center.

"We're a work in progress," declares Buckle. "We're always changing with the times. Our biggest effort currently is direct involvement with local produce growers. We have a green market set up every Saturday, where the growers sell their produce."

Standard menu items include smoothies and protein drinks; vegetarian burgers (including the signature Happy Burger); Corn Bread with Pinto Beans; Brown Rice, Guacamole, and Tossed Salad; and Vegetarian Chili Pie. There are also soups and salads.

The food is prepared using only top-quality natural ingredients — organic whenever available. All the water is purified, and macrobiotic, vegan, and low-fat menu items are always available. No hydrogenated oils are used. The menu also features a small selection of dairy, fish, and chicken dishes.

Among the most popular blackboard specials are Potatoes Curried with Chickpeas and Roasted Peppers (served over corn bread with house salad and steamed vegetables); Vegetarian Quesadillas of Grilled Tempeh (sautéed with zucchini, corn, green peppers, lemon pepper, and brown rice syrup, and served on an organic whole-wheat tortilla with black beans, avocado, and pico de gallo); and Couscous with Organic Corn (gingered lentils, daikon, and cucumber salad, organic turnips and carrots with dilled miso sauce, and organic lettuce salad).

Before or after dinner you might want to check out the natural foods store, which features everything from aromatherapy products to books and videos on healthful living.

Greek Orzo Salad

Serves 8 as a main course

The Greek Orzo Salad was selected by Suzanne Fain, co-owner with her husband, John, because "it is a very popular dish and easy to make. This salad is good as an entrée or side dish and is especially good at picnics and tailgate parties because it travels and keeps well."

1 pound orzo pasta
6 tablespoons extra-virgin olive oil
5 tablespoons white wine vinegar
1 small red onion, finely chopped
1^{1}/2 teaspoons salt
^{1}/2 teaspoon ground pepper
2 tablespoons fresh oregano
^{1}/4 cup minced fresh parsley
1 basket cherry tomatoes, halved
1 cucumber, peeled, seeded, and diced
16 Greek olives, halved and pitted
6 ounces feta cheese, crumbled

In a large pot of salted boiling water, cook pasta until al dente, 8 to 10 minutes. Drain. Place in a large serving dish and toss with 1 tablespoon olive oil.

Whisk together remaining 5 tablespoons olive oil, vinegar, onion, salt, pepper, oregano, and parsley. Pour over warm orzo. Add remaining ingredients and mix. Serve chilled or at room temperature.

Quinoa and Pine Nut Salad with Balsamic Vinaigrette

Serves 6 to 8 as a side dish

"This recipe was given to us by one of our customers, food stylist Julie Hettiger," says Suzanne. "This easy and beautiful salad is good as a main course or side dish."

4 cups water
$1/2$ teaspoon salt
2 cups quinoa
$3/4$ cup dried currants
$1/2$ cup pine nuts

BALSAMIC VINAIGRETTE
Grated zest and juice of 1 lemon
$1/4$ cup balsamic vinegar
$1/2$ teaspoon paprika
$1/2$ teaspoon ground cumin
$1/2$ teaspoon ground coriander
$3/4$ cup virgin olive oil

$1/4$ cup chopped green onions
$3/4$ cup diced red bell pepper
$3/4$ cup thinly sliced carrots
$1/2$ cup chopped fresh cilantro
2 cups of miniature yellow pear tomatoes
Mixed salad greens or green leaf lettuce for serving

In a medium saucepan, bring water to a boil. Add salt and quinoa. Cover and cook over low heat until the water is absorbed and grains have puffed up, about 10 minutes. Do not over-cook.

Drain quinoa and transfer to a large bowl. Add currants.

Meanwhile, in a dry skillet over low heat, stir pine nuts constantly until lightly toasted. Set aside.

To make the vinaigrette: in a medium bowl combine lemon zest and juice, vinegar, paprika, cumin, and coriander. Whisk in olive oil.

To quinoa, add green onions, bell pepper, carrots, cilantro, and toasted pine nuts. Add vinaigrette and toss lightly. Serve atop greens and garnish liberally with yellow pear tomatoes.

Variation: Substitute millet for half of quinoa.

HONEST OZZIE'S CAFE AND DESERT OASIS
60 North 100 West
Moab, Utah 84532
801-259-8442

OPEN DAILY 7 A.M. TO 3:30 P.M.

Price: Inexpensive to moderate
Credit cards: MC, V
Wheelchair accessible
Smoking: On patio only
Alcohol: Beer

Honest Ozzie's Cafe is a natural foods restaurant, bakery, and deli located in a historic home in the small desert town of Moab. Moab is the home of the Hollywood Stuntman's Hall of Fame as well as the gateway to popular Dead Horse State Park and Arches National Park.

The cafe, set back off the road amid ancient trees and landscaped gardens, has a facade of river rock and sandstone. The deck is the perfect spot to relax and listen to the waterfall trickling from a nearby sandstone wall. This site also affords guests a view of beautiful distant mesas and a landmark known as the Portal. The rear of the restaurant offers its own view of Honest Ozzie's organic garden and orchard.

"All and all, it's the most beautiful and serene setting in Moab," says owner Mike Macke. "And you also get healthful and delicious food at reasonable prices."

The cafe features whole-grain cereal for breakfast, and the lunch specials change daily depending on the available local organic produce. "We always have wonderful house-made desserts, soups, salads, and wraps," adds Macke.

One of the most popular lunchtime dishes is the Exotic Wrap (salmon, barbecue sauce, and pineapple fried rice, wrapped in a flour-tortilla). A best-selling salad is the Pita Salad Spread (fresh vegetables and pasta, served with spicy yogurt sauce on the side). The restaurant also brews its own beer: Honest Ale.

Chocolate-Zucchini Bread

Makes 2 large loaves

Owner Mike Macke writes: "Chocolate-Zucchini Bread is a wonderful recipe to make use of that ever-abundant summer zucchini. It can make a zucchini-lover of anyone who professes to hate the stuff.

"This bread freezes well and comes in handy for unexpected company, as a last-minute dessert, or to take on a hike. Kids love it made into muffins and iced with cream cheese. An extra tip: Grate zucchini and pack 2-cup portions in small self-sealing plastic bags and freeze. You can make bread all winter."

3/4 cup safflower oil

3 eggs

2 cups sugar

2 teaspoons vanilla extract

1 teaspoon orange extract

1/2 cup milk

2 1/2 cups all-purpose flour

1/2 cup unsweetened cocoa powder

1 teaspoon ground cinnamon

1 teaspoon salt

$1^1/2$ teaspoons baking soda

$2^1/2$ teaspoons baking powder

2 cups grated zucchini

1 cup chopped pecans

Preheat oven to 350ºF. Spray two 9-by-5-inch loaf pans or 6 mini-loaf pans with vegetable-oil cooking spray.

In a large bowl, beat oil, eggs, sugar, and vanilla together. Beat in orange extract and milk. Sift flour, cocoa, cinnamon, salt, baking soda, and baking powder together. Stir into wet ingredients until blended. Stir in zucchini and nuts until blended.

Pour into prepared pans. Bake large loaves 55 to 60 minutes and mini-loaves 25 to 30 minutes, or until a toothpick inserted in center comes out clean. Do not overbake; breads should be moist. Let cool in pans for 10 minutes. Unmold and let cool completely on wire racks.

MORNING RAY CAFE AND BAKERY
268 Main Street
Park City, Utah 84036
435-649-5686

OPEN DAILY 7 A.M. TO 3 P.M.

Price: Inexpensive to moderate
Credit cards: AE, MC, V
No wheelchair access
No smoking
Alcohol: 3.2 beer

Morning Ray Cafe and Bakery is housed in a Park City building dating back to the 1900s. The wood-framed building was extensively renovated in 1988. Park City was once a mining town, and the restaurant is located near the top of its historic Main Street.

Today, the area boasts three ski resorts and plenty of hiking. It's a great place to mountain bike during the summer months. The restaurant's many windows front on Main Street and bathe the cheery dining room with natural light.

Morning Ray was originally located a few doors up the street and specialized mostly in baked goods. In those days, the cafe was so small there wasn't even room for a kitchen. Owners Paula McGee and her husband, Paul Woods, used commercial kitchens for their baking and food preparation.

Nowadays, in its new location, the cafe's own kitchen is the source of the hearty breakfasts, tasty lunches, and fine baked goods that the Morning Ray has become famous for.

The cafe's reputation has spread, thanks to a spate of national publicity. Usually bustling in the mornings, it is a casual and comfortable eatery for both locals and out-of-towners. In addition to table and booth seating, a coffee bar overlooking Main Street is a perfect site for people-watching.

Breakfast favorites include the croissants, cheese danish, cinnamon rolls, and huevos rancheros (available with tofu instead of eggs).

Other popular breakfast dishes are the Morning Ray (home fries with veggies, cheese, sour cream, and guacamole), fluffy omelets, organic buckwheat-cornmeal hotcakes, and authentic sourdough hotcakes made with an Alaskan sourdough starter that is well over 100 years old.

Favorite lunch dishes include the Organic Bean Burger, the Artichoke Croissant Sandwich with melted Jarlsberg cheese, and Baba G's Favorite (baba ghanouj with sautéed vegetables served in pita bread). A variety of vegetarian soups are also quite popular.

A full list of house-made desserts feature such decadent sweets as Dreambars, brownies, biscotti, cheesecakes, and tortes.

Huevos Rancheros

Serves 4 to 6 as a main course

Paula McGee says that because she is of Mexican descent, she knows how to make a "mean" huevos rancheros.

"This has become one of our most popular items, reflecting the Western character of our region. It is high in protein, easily prepared at home, and can be varied to please many different palates."

6 ounces soft silken tofu or 6 eggs
1/4 cup green onions, chopped
4 to 6 whole-wheat or white-flour tortillas
2 to 3 cups cooked black or pinto beans, refried and seasoned as desired
4 to 6 ounces shredded jack cheese
Guacamole, sour cream (optional), alfalfa sprouts, salsa, and pickled jalapeno
    chilies for garnish

In a large skillet, over medium heat, scramble together tofu or eggs and onions until fluffy. Keep warm.

In a large skillet over medium heat, heat tortilla quickly on both sides. Spread with 1/2 cup warm beans, top with 3 ounces tofu mixture or eggs, and top with cheese.

Cover pan and allow cheese to melt, or put on a plate and melt under a broiler. Garnish with guacamole, optional sour cream, and sprouts. Serve salsa and jalapenos on the side.

PARK IVY GARDEN CAFE
878 South 900 East
Salt Lake City, Utah 84102
801-318-1313

OPEN MONDAY THROUGH SATURDAY 11 A.M. TO 9 P.M.

Price: Inexpensive
Credit cards: AE, MC, V
Wheelchair accessible
No smoking
No alcohol

This warm and inviting restaurant has won several awards for best vegetarian restaurant, including a recent one from *Vegetarian Gourmet* magazine.

Chef-owner Mark Machlis believes that it is his mission to "strive to maintain great food and service." A firm believer in the vegetarian way of life, Mark argues that the best way to gain more converts is by "catering to taste first, health second."

It's a philosophy that seems to be working. Diners who flock to this popular fifty-five-seat restaurant — including many nonvegetarians — rave about its cozy, nourishing atmosphere, excellent service, and wonderful healthy food.

The restaurant's interior has an indoor-garden look, with ivy-covered trellises, track lighting, exposed brick walls, and cozy nooks that afford guests privacy.

But, the real secret to the Park Ivy Garden Cafe's success is an imaginative and varied menu of reasonably priced healthy dishes.

Popular menu items include Sausage-Style Hash Browns, Meat-of-Wheat Loaf, Save the Chicken Salad, Burritos, Meatless Burger, Lasagna (with artichoke hearts, chickpeas, and spinach) and the cafe's freshly baked Sunbun Bread.

Many of the specials offered have international accents, such as the Mexican-style Milagro Bean Field and the vegetarian Japanese sushi made with jicama (a crunchy, sweet root vegetable). Also exceptional are the salad dressings, with flavors like raspberry, cucumber, and rosemary.

All the pastries, muffins, and other baked goods are all made from organic flour and are egg-free. There is also an excellent selection of dairy-free baked goods.

If you're not too hungry, light lunch entrées are available either to eat in or take out.

Raspberry "Chicken"

Serves 10 as a main course

The Raspberry "Chicken" is one of the restaurant's all-time favorites, according to owner Mark Machlis. "Fresh raspberries and flavored vinegar are only a hint of what makes this dish a gourmet experience. It's a versatile entrée that can be served warm over cooked rice or pasta, or mixed with chilled pasta to create a cold raspberry-'chicken' salad."

$1/2$ cup minced shallots
$1/2$ cup finely chopped carrots
$1/4$ cup finely chopped celery
$3 1/2$ cups fresh or thawed frozen raspberries
$1/4$ cup brandy
$1/4$ cup raspberry vinegar

1¹/2 cups Sucanat or packed brown sugar

2 tablespoons minced fresh tarragon, or 2 teaspoons dried tarragon

2 tablespoons minced fresh mint

3 pounds chicken substitute, diced (about 6 cups) available in health foods stores

Spray a large skillet with vegetable-oil cooking spray. Heat over medium heat and sauté shallots, carrots, and celery until browned, about 8 minutes. Set aside.

In a blender or food processor, puree raspberries. Strain puree through a fine-meshed sieve and discard seeds. Pour puree into a large bowl. Add brandy, vinegar, and Sucanat or brown sugar and mix well. Stir raspberry mixture into vegetables and add herbs. Stir in chicken substitute, cover, and simmer over low heat until almost all liquid is absorbed, about 20 minutes.

Vegetable Lasagna

Serves 10 as a main course

"This delicious lasagna is a creative combination of artichoke hearts, chickpeas, and spinach," says Mark. "Since it weighs in at only 6 grams of fat per serving, everybody can indulge!"

VEGETABLE MIXTURE

12 ounces fresh spinach, stemmed and chopped (about 10 cups)

1 zucchini, finely diced

1 yellow squash, finely diced

2 carrots, finely diced

1/2 cup finely chopped artichoke hearts

2 cups cooked chickpeas, rinsed and drained

CHEESE MIXTURE

6 cups nonfat cottage cheese

2 tablespoons minced fresh basil, or 2 teaspoons dried

1 tablespoon minced fresh oregano, or 1 teaspoon dried oregano

$1/2$ teaspoon each salt and ground pepper

1 tablespoon powdered egg product

1 pound dried lasagna noodles

$3/4$ cup tomato sauce

$1/2$ cup water

2 cups (8 ounces) shredded part-skim mozzarella cheese

To make vegetable mixture: Steam spinach, drain, and squeeze out water. Chop and place in a large bowl with remaining ingredients. Set aside.

To make cheese mixture: Combine all ingredients in a large bowl. Set aside.

In a large pot of salted boiling water, cook lasagna noodles until al dente, 8 to 10 minutes. Drain.

Preheat oven to 300°F. In a small bowl, mix tomato sauce and water. Spread $1/4$ cup of sauce evenly in a lasagna pan. Place a layer of noodles over sauce. Spread half of cheese mixture over noodles, followed by $1/2$ cup of sauce and half of mozzarella. Repeat layering, except for remaining mozzarella.

Bake, uncovered, for 45 minutes. Cover pan with aluminum foil and bake 45 minutes longer. Uncover and sprinkle with remaining mozzarella. Bake, uncovered, until cheese is melted, about 5 minutes. Remove from oven and let sit for 15 minutes before cutting and serving.

Sausage-Style Hash Browns

Serves 4 as a side dish

Mark advises: "If you're in need of some down-home comfort, try this popular dish. Serve it with oven-fresh biscuits and vegetarian gravy."

2 pounds boiling potatoes, finely diced
1 onion, finely chopped
1 garlic clove, minced
$1/2$ cup finely chopped green bell pepper
1 tablespoon dry sherry or water
8 ounces soy sausage or other sausage substitute
Salt and freshly ground pepper to taste
1 tablespoon minced fresh dill, or 1 teaspoon dried dill
1 tablespoon chopped fresh cilantro (optional)

Preheat oven to 450°F. Spray an ovenproof casserole with vegetable-oil cooking spray and set aside.

Place potatoes in a large saucepan with salted cold water to cover. Bring to a boil and cook for 10 minutes; drain and set aside.

In a medium saucepan, sauté onion, garlic, and bell pepper in sherry or water until onion is translucent, about 5 minutes. Stir in sausage substitute, potatoes, and remaining ingredients. Transfer to casserole dish and bake until browned, about 15 minutes.

HORN OF THE MOON CAFE
8 Langdon Street
Montpelier, Vermont 05602
802-223-2895

OPEN TUESDAY THROUGH SATURDAY 7 A.M. TO 9 P.M., SUNDAY 9 A.M. TO 9 P.M.

Price: Moderate to expensive
No credit cards
No wheelchair access
No smoking
Alcohol: Beer and wine

Established in 1977 and located in the small Vermont town of Montpelier, the Horn of the Moon Cafe is the oldest vegetarian restaurant in New England.

A popular hangout for local artists, businessmen, and politicians, it's also quite popular with the tourist trade. Owner Gary Beardsworth describes his establishment, located in an old building overlooking the North Branch River, as "very funky. It hasn't changed much over the years."

Walk in and you're greeted by the tantalizing aromas of bread baking and soups cooking. The ceilings are high, with large windows. The cafe is adorned with green plants and the work of area artists in a rotating exhibit.

For the politically minded diner, shelves overflowing with leaflets announce political movements and actions. A bulletin board is filled with notices ranging from classes being offered to dances.

Vegan and heart-healthy dishes are indicated on the menu, and organic produce and ingredients are used whenever possible. The menu lists home-made breads, soups, salads, sandwiches and daily specials.

Among the many favorite dishes are Tofu-Mushroom Stroganoff, stir-fries, Hornikopita, and Veggie-Rice Burgers. For breakfast-lovers, there are Honey Wheatgerm Pancakes, Scrambled Tofu, Cinnamon Vanilla French Toast, omelettes, and fresh muffins.

Thai Hot Mustard Stirfry

Serves 4 as a main course

STIRFRY INGREDIENTS

tofu, tempeh or seitan, green or red peppers, carrots, celery, onions, broccoli, snow peas, kale, mushrooms, bean sprouts

SAUCE

4 cloves garlic, minced

$1/2$ walnut-sized piece of ginger root, minced

$3/4$ cup orange juice

1 tablespoon orange peel, minced

$1/4$ cup cider vinegar

$1/4$ cup honey

1 tablespoon prepared mustard

$1 1/2$ teaspoon chili peppers

1 tablespoon arrowroot or cornstarch

To make the sauce: mix all ingredients, except arrowroot, together. Mix the arrowroot with 2 tablespoons of the sauce and stir to remove any lumps. Add back to the sauce.

Stirfry: Choose six or eight of the stir fry ingredients; cut into bite-sized pieces. Add the hardest vegetables to your hot oil first. Cook quickly at high heart, 4 to 5 minutes, until all ingredients are hot but crisp. Add sauce and cook until thickened, about 1 minute. Add first: tofu, tempeh or seitan, green pepper or red pepper, carrot, celery, onion, broccoli, snow peas, and kale. Add second: mushrooms and bean sprouts.

DOE BAY CAFE
Star Route 86
Olga, Washington 98279
360-376-2577/2291

SUMMER: OPEN DAILY 7:30 A.M. TO 9:30 P.M. WINTER: OPEN SATURDAY AND SUNDAY 8 TO 11 A.M. FOR BREAK-FAST AND 6 TO 9 P.M. FOR DINNER.

Price: Moderate
Credit cards: AE, D, MC, V
Wheelchair accessible
No smoking
Alcohol: Wine and beer

Wood floors and benches, a cozy wood stove in cold weather, and a fantastic view of Otter Cove and the neighboring San Juan Islands gives this casual cafe a rustic, charming, and relaxed atmosphere.

The cafe is housed in a turn-of-the-century building in the historic Doe Bay Village Resort and Retreat on Orcas Island. Butcher-block paper and crayons on the tables inspire patrons to create art that can be hung on the walls. Outdoor seating is available during the summer months so that diners can enjoy the fresh Pacific breezes and gorgeous views.

Working up an appetite in this part of the world is easy. The area features guided kayak trips, hiking trails, and many other vigorous activities. After all that exercise, there are cedar saunas and hot tubs to ease aching muscles.

The set menu (which is expanded during the busy tourist season) is vegetarian, and everything is "made from scratch with love." Fresh seafood specials are featured each day, along with special vegetarian entrées, homemade breads, and desserts.

Early-morning favorites include the Breakfast Burrito (scrambled eggs, home fries, peppers, cheeses, and black bean chili wrapped in a tortilla and topped with salsa and sour cream) and the Homemade Granola.

For dinner, try the popular Stir-Fry (vegetables served over brown rice with spicy Thai peanut or ginger sauce with seared tofu) or Eggplant Parmesan (broiled eggplant layered with walnut-ricotta cream and served over pasta marinara).

Organically raised local and seasonal products are used when available, and the wine list features a mostly Northwest selection.

Grilled Portobello Mushroom Sandwiches

Serves 2 as a main course

According to Doe Bay's baker, Bev Simko, the Grilled Portobello Sandwich "is a seasonal favorite that *overwhelmingly* seems to please both meat eaters and vegetarians alike."

1 very large, very fresh portobello mushroom, stemmed

MARINADE
1/4 cup balsamic vinegar
1 garlic clove, minced
3 tablespoons olive oil
Salt and freshly cracked pepper to taste
1 tablespoon minced fresh herbs

BLUE CHEESE SAUCE
2 tablespoons crumbled blue cheese
2 tablespoons mayonnaise
$1/2$ teaspoons vegetarian Worcestershire sauce
2 tablespoons buttermilk
Pinch of salt and freshly ground pepper to taste
Minced fresh parsley to taste

2 crusty sandwich rolls, halved
Mixed salad greens
Thinly sliced red onion

Light a fire in a charcoal grill, or preheat a gas grill or broiler. Slice portobello into 1-inch-thick horizontal strips. Combine all ingredients for marinade and toss with mushroom slices. Whisk together all ingredients for blue cheese sauce.

Grill or broil mushrooms for 5 minutes, or until tender. Just before removing mushrooms from grill, brush both sides of rolls with remaining marinade and lightly toast on grill or under broiler.

Place rolls open-faced on serving plates. Place mixed greens and red onion slices on top half, and grilled mushroom slices on the bottom half of roll. Top mushroom slices with blue cheese sauce to taste. Serve with herbed lemony potato wedges, as we do at the restaurant, if you like.

GRAVITY BAR
415 Broadway Avenue East
Seattle, Washington 98102
206-325-7186

OPEN SUNDAY THROUGH THURSDAY 10 A.M. TO 10 P.M., FRIDAY AND SATURDAY UNTIL 11 P.M.

Price: Inexpensive to moderate
No credit cards
Wheelchair accessible, but seats and tables are high
No smoking
No alcohol

The crowd is young, the neighborhood is trendy, and the decor high-tech futuristic but with a human touch. According to owner Laurrien Gilman, the decor of the Gravity Bar is "designed to augment and enhance the foods that we serve."

The galvanized metal cone-shaped tables are lit from within, so that the food placed on the tables is bathed in light. The restaurant's bar, or counter, is also lit from within and illuminates the faces of the customers who are seated there. Behind the counter, mounds of fruits and vegetables come alive with light.

"The effect is ethereal. The beauty and the spirits of people and food shine," Gilman says.

Besides shining, the simple but elegant food at this natural foods restaurant is also delicious. And the selection is extensive, featuring raw, vegan, and macrobiotic choices. The

Gravity Bar uses organic ingredients and produce whenever possible.

For late risers, breakfast is available until 2 P.M. A breakfast crowd favorite is Scrambled Eggs with Vegetables, or Tofu Scramble. For lunch or dinner, popular specials are Hummus Roll-Up (hummus, parsley, tomatoes, green peppers, sprouts, and carrots rolled up in a whole-wheat tortilla), and New Doctor Gravity Choice (a bowl of rice with marinated tofu, sprouts, tomatoes, and lemon tahini, served with buckwheat toast).

Desserts are usually vegan, and include cookies and cakes. A favorite pick is the Chocolate Inca Cake.

Equinox Salad

Serves 4 as an appetizer

"I selected the Equinox Salad for this book because I feel it has very healthful and balanced properties," explains owner Laurrien Gilman. "It contains fresh, raw vegetables, with a moderate amount of grain for protein.

"A touch of cheese is used as a seasoning and for added protein, and the Lemon-Flax Dressing is full of flavor and nutrition. Flaxseed oil contains omega-3, and is one of the essential fatty acids that many vegetarians lack.

"The safflower oil contains omega-6, and together they form a very complete oil. In my way of thinking, fat is not bad, and therefore low-fat is not better. What is largely overlooked in this realm is the importance of *quality fats* that the body must have to be healthy and function optimally. (It is also a misunderstanding that by eating fats, we get fat).

"This salad is very satisfying, with balanced protein, carbohydrates, and fats (while not heavy on the fat). I find that meals in this category both satisfy the palate and the body's needs."

2 cups quinoa
Pinch of salt
3 cups water

4 cups mixed salad greens (including any of these: romaine, red or white chard,
    kale, spinach)
2 cups grated carrots
$1/2$ cup crumbled feta cheese
$1/2$ cup finely chopped green onions
1 cup diced Roma (plum) tomatoes

LEMON-FLAX DRESSING
Makes about $1^1/3$ cups

$1/4$ cup cold-pressed flaxseed oil
$1/4$ cup safflower oil
$1/2$ cup fresh lemon juice
$1/4$ cup soy sauce
3 tablespoons nutritional yeast
2 tablespoons crushed garlic

In a large saucepan, combine quinoa, salt, and water. Bring to a boil, then reduce heat, cover
and simmer for 40 minutes, or until tender.

On large plates, make a bed of greens and nest 1 cup of quinoa in center. Surround quinoa
with grated carrots. Top quinoa with feta. Sprinkle green onions over carrots and tomatoes
over greens. Ladle $1/3$ cup dressing over each serving.

To make dressing: In a blender combine all ingredients and puree. Stir before using.

MOUNTAIN PEOPLE'S KITCHEN
1400 University Avenue
Morgantown, West Virginia 26505
304-291-6131

OPEN FOR BREAKFAST AND LUNCH MONDAY THROUGH THURSDAY 9 A.M. TO 4 P.M., LUNCH ONLY SATURDAY 11 A.M. TO 4 P.M.; DINNER MONDAY THROUGH THURSDAY 5 TO 8 P.M.; BRUNCH SUNDAY 10 A.M. TO 2 P.M

Price: Inexpensive to moderate
Credit cards: D, MC, V
Wheelchair accessible
No smoking
No alcohol

Nestled among the hilly streets of Morgantown, West Virginia, is an oasis called the Mountain People's Kitchen, attached to a natural foods cooperative and located just two blocks from West Virginia University.

The kitchen has been serving up the only vegetarian fare in this town since 1990, so assistant manager Kelly Fritz has proclaimed it "Mo-town's premiere vegetarian restaurant." The food here is delicious, nutritious, and affordable and is served in generous portions.

Since the restaurant is located smack in the middle of Morgantown's business district, guests in suits and ties or blue jeans and T-shirts vie for seats. The courteous staff treats everyone alike. "Our staff is ever-so-helpful in turning patrons on to a new vegetarian delight," Fritz states.

The cafe's casual, eclectic interior features an ever-changing art exhibition, with openings every six to eight weeks.

In addition to daily soups and specials, the menu features a full selection of salads, sandwiches, and entrées. Brunch is featured on Sundays. There are nondairy options, and organically grown foods are used when available. Almost any special dietary need can be met on request.

A popular favorite is the Burger of the Day (Tofu Garden Vegetable and Lentil Walnut are just two of the delicious possibilities). Customers rave about the hummus (Mideastern Chickpea Salad), Veggie Melt, and Sesame Noodles with Grilled Tofu.

Banana Chocolate Chip Muffins

Makes 1 dozen muffins

"Bananas always seem to be one of the most abundant and versatile fruits to bake with," says Fritz. "As for our Banana Chocolate Chip Muffins, I decided that our original plain old banana nut muffin needed some new character.

"While gazing around the kitchen at the various ingredients that could be used, one caught my eye. Sitting all by itself on the top shelf was a bag of chocolate chips!

"Almost instantly, the creative nerves in my body began to awake. Why not chocolate chips in muffins? Why not bananas combined with chocolate chips in muffins? A baking marriage was about to unfold. Forty-five minutes later we were sampling the results of this successful experiment.

"Today, it's the most popular muffin served in the restaurant, no one can resist eating one. So, whether it's a cup of coffee or a glass of (soy) milk, Banana Chocolate Chip Muffins are the perfect complement to your next luncheon or dinner party.

2 cups all-purpose flour
1 teaspoon baking powder
1 teaspoon ground cinnamon
$^1/_2$ cup canola oil
1 cup turbinado sugar or Sucanat
2 eggs or pasteurized egg product equivalent
1 teaspoon vanilla extract
1 to 1$^1/_2$ cups mashed bananas
$^1/_2$ to $^3/_4$ cup chocolate chips

Preheat oven to 350ºF. Grease 12 muffin cups. In a medium bowl, combine flour, baking powder, and cinnamon.

In a large bowl, combine oil, turbinado or Sucanat, eggs or egg product equivalent, and vanilla. Add bananas and chocolate chips and mix well.

Add dry mixture to wet mixture and stir until just mixed. Fill prepared muffin cups three-fourths full. Bake for 20 to 25 minutes, or until lightly browned. Let cool slightly and unmold. Serve warm.

BEANS AND BARLEY
1901 East North Avenue
Milwaukee, Wisconsin 53202
414-278-7878

OPEN DAILY 9 A.M. TO 9 P.M.

Price: Moderate
Credit cards: MC, V
Wheelchair accessible
No smoking
Alcohol: Beer and wine

For more than 6 years, the owners of Beans and Barley watched customers shop in their popular natural foods store and asked themselves one question: "Are they hungry?"

They learned the answer when they decided to expand their small east-side neighborhood shop in 1979 to include food service. The seventy-seat deli/cafe went on to become one of the most popular natural foods eateries in the city.

When a fire gutted the old location, they decided that it was time for a larger place. The new Beans and Barley opened its doors in 1994, in an 18,000-square-foot building on North Avenue.

Co-owner Pat Sturgis jokingly describes the architectural design of Beans and Barley, which features curved majestic lines and 23-foot-high ceilings, as a cross between the "Jetsons and futuristic." "The architecture is the decor," he states.

In this light and airy modern building, you can buy vitamins or shampoo, then take home a slice of pie, cake, or tart. Or, you can grab a table and have a hot or cold salad or one of the other delicious entrées served in the cafe.

"Our goal is more than just nutrition — more than just the right vitamins or selling good domestic cheese," Pat proclaims. "Our aim is also to see that you're well fed."

The cafe and deli features vegetarian, Mexican, Middle Eastern, and Italian specialties. Organic products are used whenever possible, and vegan options are available. There is no red meat to be found here.

Beans and Barley is best known for its burritos, but another favorite is lasagna (pasta, spinach pesto, ground turkey, ragu, and cheese). Also a popular item is Beautiful Broccoli (a salad of carrots, bell peppers, and broccoli in a raspberry-sesame vinaigrette).

Reviews in local newspapers have raved about the cafes soups as well as its (alas, not low-fat) desserts. The Four-Layer Poppy Seed Torte is to die for, and the cafe can hardly keep up with the demand for its Blueberry Pie during the summer months. The pie is nondairy and made with honey instead of sugar.

Tarascan Bean Soup

Serves 6 to 8 as an appetizer

The Tarascan Bean Soup and Smoked Turkey and Swiss Sandwich are offered by owner Pat Sturgis because "it's a typical Beans and Barley combination: a little international home cooking — this one from Mexico — and, because we don't serve red meat, our adaptation of a favorite American sandwich, grilled ham and cheese."

3 cups dried pinto beans
1^{1}/2 cups diced onions
5 cups cold vegetable stock

1 tablespoon salt
28 ounces canned whole tomatoes
28 ounces canned diced tomatoes
1 teaspoon minced garlic
1 tablespoon ground cumin
$1/2$ teaspoon cayenne pepper
$1/2$ teaspoon ground coriander
$1/4$ cup tamari soy sauce
Sour cream and fresh cilantro for garnish

Rinse and pick over beans. Soak overnight in water to cover by 2 inches. Drain. In a soup pot, combine beans, onions, stock, and salt. Bring to a boil, reduce heat to simmer, cover, and cook until tender, about $1^{1}/2$ hours. In a blender or food processor, in batches if necessary, puree beans until smooth.

In a large saucepan, combine all remaining ingredients except sour cream and cilantro and bring to a boil. Cook for 5 minutes. Add bean mixture and heat through. Serve garnished with a dollop of sour cream and a sprinkle of cilantro.

Grilled Turkey and Cheese Sandwich

Serves 1 as a main course

2 slices light rye bread
Dijon mustard for spreading
Sliced smoked turkey breast
Sliced Swiss cheese
1 teaspoon butter, melted
Sliced tomatoes and dill pickle for serving

Spread 1 slice of bread with mustard. Add turkey and cheese. Top with second bread slice. Brush top and bottom of sandwich with melted butter. Heat a medium skillet over medium-hot heat. Add sandwich, cover, and cook for 3 minutes, or until golden brown. Turn, cover, and cook until golden brown on second side, about 3 minutes. Serve with tomatoes and dill pickle alongside.

SUNROOM RESTAURANT
638 State Street
Madison, Wisconsin 53703
608-255-1555

Open daily 7 a.m. to 10 p.m.

Price: Moderate
Credit cards: MC, V
No wheelchair access
No smoking
Alcohol: Wine and beer

Tucked away on the second floor in the back of an old building, the Sunroom Restaurant is a quiet getaway from the hustle and bustle of Madison's main street and the monolithic University of Wisconsin located only a few steps away.

There's a casual, clean feel to this European-style cafe with wooden tables and hardwood floors. Large windows let in lots of light and create an open feeling to the room. The streaming light enhances the work of local artists that is displayed on the walls.

The menu features mostly international vegetarian cuisine, but some chicken dishes can be found here. Owner Mark Paradise states that the cafe's Vegetarian Chili is the best, and a very popular choice among the mostly student crowd.

Another favorite to be found at this natural foods restaurant, which utilizes some organic produce, is the meatless made-to-order pasta. The Pasta Ciociara (a sauce of black olives, tomatoes, green peppers, wine, and garlic served over angel hair or penne rigate) is a winner, as is the Mediterranean Pasta.

There is a bakery on the premises, and the cafe is widely known for its gourmet desserts. The Apple-Pecan Upside-Down Pie and Carrot Cake are only two examples of these irresistible sweet-tooth satisfiers.

Greek Shrimp Pasta

Serves 2 as main course

The Greek Shrimp Pasta is "an impressive-looking dish that will wow a dinner guest," promises owner Mark Paradise. "The combination of the feta cheese, tomatoes, and white wine is what makes this such a tasty dish."

2 tablespoons virgin olive oil

2 teaspoons minced garlic

4 green onions, cut into $1/2$-inch pieces

$3/4$ cup dry white wine

6 ripe tomatoes or 8 Roma (plum) tomatoes, peeled, seeded, and chopped

3 to 4 fresh basil leaves

10 medium shrimp, peeled and deveined

6 ounces feta cheese, crumbled

Minced fresh parsley to garnish

Fettuccine for serving

Cook pasta in a large pot of salted boiling water until al dente, 8 to 10 minutes. Drain.

In a large saucepan over medium heat, heat oil and sauté garlic and green onions until garlic turns a light golden brown. Add wine, tomatoes, and basil and cook until tomatoes are tender. Add shrimp and cook until pink and opaque, 3 to 4 minutes. Add feta cheese, reserving some to sprinkle on top. Toss hot pasta with sauce. Serve sprinkled with reserved cheese and parsley.

GOVINDA'S VEGETARIAN GARDEN RESTAURANT
South Slope, South East Drive
Burnaby, British Columbia
V3J 7W2 Canada
604-433-2428

OPEN DAILY 11:30 A.M. TO 8:30 P.M.

Price: Moderate
Credit cards: MC, V
Wheelchair accessible
No smoking
No alcohol

Colorfully-robed members of the Hari Krishna movement operate Govinda restaurants all over the world and the Burnaby location has one of their most bucolic settings.

The vegetarian garden and patio restaurant is located on ten acres of beautiful parkland and is surrounded by flowers and trees. For casual dining with a spiritual theme, this is the place to go. Located on the grounds is an authentic Vedic temple, where you are free to meditate.

Enhancing the peaceful atmosphere is a waterfall — a wonderful place to eat your lunch — or you can dine under the stars (May through October) in the outdoor seating area. Both indoor and outdoor dining areas seat thirty.

Manager Pat Charnelle describes the restaurant's interior as very restful, with an indoor-garden feel to it. "There's lots of wood paneling, and overhead fans that turn slowly and give the room a soft atmosphere." Large windows overlooking the vegetarian garden dominate three sides of the dining room.

Govinda's offers a "karma-free" diet, including a full buffet of Indian and Western dishes. There are three subjis (hot vegetable preparations) featured each day, along with a full salad bar, two kinds of rice, and lentil soup. Popular dinner entrées include lasagna, quiche, and eggplant Parmesan, while the samosa is an ever-popular appetizer.

This vegetarian restaurant uses organically raised foods when available. It is also famous for its Indian sweets and savories, such as halvah with fresh fruit salad.

Although prices at Govinda's are consistently reasonable, the all-you-can-eat buffet lunch is a special value. Desserts are not included, but are well worth the extra price.

Spinach and Yogurt Salad (Palak Ka Raita)

Serves 6 to 8 as a side dish

Pat Charnelle describes the Spinach and Yogurt Salad (palak ka raita) as "a cooling dish for summer that is always a favorite choice among customers."

1 pound fresh spinach, washed and stemmed

2 cups plain yogurt

1 teaspoon cumin seeds, toasted and ground

$1/2$ teaspoon garam masala

$1/4$ teaspoon ground pepper

1 teaspoon salt

Plunge spinach leaves into a saucepan of boiling water for 1 to 2 minutes to wilt them. Drain, press out excess water with the back of a large spoon, and chop coarsely.

In a large bowl, combine spinach and remaining ingredients. Mix with a fork. Serve warm or cold with pori (fried bread) or as a refreshing side dish to an elaborate meal.

THE NAAM RESTAURANT
2724 West Fourth Avenue
Vancouver, British Columbia
V6K 1R1 Canada
604-738-7151

OPEN 24 HOURS DAILY

Price: Moderate
Credit cards: AE, IN, MC, V
Wheelchair accessible
No smoking
Alcohol: Local beer on tap, wine, hard cider

A vintage clapboard building on what used to be called Rainbow Road houses Vancouver's oldest natural foods restaurant. Still thriving after 25 years of operation, the Naam Restaurant recently won the Readers' Choice Award from *Vancouver Magazine* as the best vegetarian restaurant in the city.

The coffeehouse decor is as close to Alice's Restaurant as you can get, complete with folk singers at dinner, a piano player at lunch, and Joni Mitchell on the juke box. The Naam is a meat-free, smoke-free environment, and if you look hard enough, you might even find a faded "End the War in Vietnam" sticker in a corner of the room.

Here, you can enjoy the crackle of an open fireplace in winter and relax on the garden patio during warm weather — whether or not you are a vegetarian. In fact, co-owner Peter

Keith and partner Bob Woodsworth claim the restaurant draws a good number of nonveg-etarians. "I'd say there are a lot of people who come here, just because it's a healthy atmos-phere and the food is good," Peter asserts.

The restaurant is open around the clock every day of the year except Christmas. You can start your day here with an early-morning breakfast of Naam Porridge (granola and blue-berries) or Naam Steak and Eggs (a meatless patty smothered with miso gravy, two eggs any style, and fries).

The Naam features daily specials, which are chalked on a blackboard. Vegan, macrobi-otic, and nondairy options are available. One of the most popular lunchtime plates is the Naam Burger Deluxe (grilled tofu with beets and walnuts served on a whole-wheat sesame bun with tomatoes and sprouts). Try a side of Sesame Fries, with a miso "gravy."

Dinner favorites include Spinach Enchiladas (open-faced corn tortillas with spinach, onions, yogurt, and hot sauce, topped with melted cheese) and Tofu Teriyaki (organic tofu with stir-fried veggies, teriyaki sauce, and almonds, served with brown rice).

For dessert, the Double Fudge Chocolate Cake is a winner, and the Apple Crisp is pure delight. A nice selection of after-dinner herbal teas includes Mama Naam (strawberry leaf, nettle, licorice root, and rose petals).

Apple Crisp

Serves 6 as a dessert

"Our Apple Crisp recipe is one of the secrets of our success," Peter Keith says. "Our patrons keep coming back for it! It's easy to make, everybody loves it, and it's one of the few desserts that most people will appreciate.

"Apple crisp is timeless. It's like oatmeal cookies, and raisin bran muffins. Really. It's just plain good."

8 apples, cored and sliced
1 teaspoon ground cinnamon
$^1/_3$ cup honey
2 tablespoons whole-wheat flour
$^2/_3$ cup raisins
1 cup apple juice
Juice of 1 lemon

TOPPING
$1^1/_2$ cups old-fashioned rolled oats
$^1/_3$ cup wheat germ
$^2/_3$ cup whole-wheat pastry flour
$^2/_3$ cup packed brown sugar
$^1/_4$ cup chopped almonds
$^1/_3$ cup sunflower seeds
$1^1/_2$ teaspoons ground cinnamon
$^1/_3$ teaspoon salt
$^1/_3$ cup butter

Preheat oven to 350ºF. In a large bowl, combine apples, cinnamon, honey, flour, raisins, apple juice, and lemon juice. Pour into a 9-inch square baking dish.

To make topping: In a medium bowl, combine all topping ingredients except butter. Cut in butter or margarine until soft and crumbly. Sprinkle over apple mixture.

Cover with aluminum foil and bake for 45 minutes, or until apples are bubbly. Remove foil and bake for 10 minutes or until golden.

WOODLANDS NATURAL FOODS RESTAURANT
2582 West Broadway
Vancouver, British Columbia
V6K 2G1 Canada
604-733-5411

OPEN MONDAY THROUGH THURSDAY 6:30 A.M. TO 10 P.M., FRIDAY AND SATURDAY 6:30 A.M. TO 11 P.M., SUNDAY 8 A.M. TO 10 P.M.

Price: Moderate
Credit cards: AE, MC, V
Wheelchair accessible
No smoking
Alcohol: Beer and wine

For an idea of what this popular Vancouver natural foods restaurant looks like, imagine an exotic indoor garden setting. Different varieties of plants, collected over the years, grow everywhere, and the restaurant is divided into bi-level seating areas. If you prefer to dine alfresco, on summer days or evenings, you can sit and enjoy a delicious meal on the deck.

The food at Woodlands is truly international, with dishes ranging from sushi and tortillas to basmati rice, Greek moussaka, pastas, and lasagna. All entrées are free of meat, fish, fowl, and eggs.

Woodlands' president, Ragu Lehder, explains that the food served here reflects his idea of a healthy diet. "In order to live a healthy vegetarian life, you have to eat the right combination of vegetables, beans, and protein sources like milk, tofu, yogurt. I trust our restaurant is giving its customers ideas about how to create that combination — and with an appealing taste."

The restaurant also caters to guests who have special dietary needs by providing wheat-free and dairy-free dishes. Nutritional information about each dish is displayed on the specials board in order to give guests a better understanding of the food offered.

At Woodlands, the food is displayed on hot-and-cold buffets, with fifteen to twenty items to choose from. Customers are charged for their meals by weight. Organically raised products are utilized whenever possible, and beverages range from organic coffee to herbal teas and organic juices.

For breakfast-lovers, the unique combinations seem endless — from a variety of tofu dishes to hot cereals, waffles, and Indian specialties. The restaurant operates its own bakery and is proud of its "eggless baking." Here, you can enjoy the baked goods and desserts featured on the menu without worrying about fat or cholesterol.

Peas and Paneer

Serves 2 as a main course

Owner Ragu Lehder describes Peas and Paneer (house-made cheese) as an extremely popular dish. "This Indian curry was first served in our restaurant on the day it opened, and has been served here ever since."

MASALA
1/2 cup (1 stick) butter
1/2 white onion, finely chopped
1/4 teaspoon ground turmeric
1/4 teaspoon cayenne pepper

1 large ripe tomato, finely chopped
2 to 4 ounces grated fresh ginger

PANEER
1 quart milk
$1/4$ cup buttermilk

$1^1/2$ cups fresh or frozen green peas
$1/2$ cup water
Steamed rice, chapati, or pita bread for serving

To make masala: In a large saucepan, melt butter over medium heat and cook onion until lightly browned. Add turmeric, cayenne, tomato, and ginger, and cook, stirring frequently, for 5 to 10 minutes, or until butter separates from tomato and onion. Set aside.

To make paneer: In a medium saucepan, bring milk to a boil. Add buttermilk, which will clabber the hot milk. Line a large sieve with muslin or 2 thicknesses of cheesecloth and sit it over a bowl. Pour milk mixture through the sieve and let fully drain. Wrap paneer in cloth and set a heavy weight on top to press it into a flat disk. Let sit for about 1 hour. Cut into small cubes and set aside.

Cook peas in salted boiling water until tender. Drain and add to masala. Stir in water and cook over medium heat for several minutes, stirring frequently.

Add paneer and cook about 2 minutes. Serve with rice, chapati, or pita bread.

SATISFACTION FEAST VEGETARIAN RESTAURANT
1581 Grafton Street
Halifax, Nova Scotia
B3J 2C3 Canada
902-422-3540

OPEN DAILY 8 A.M. TO 9:30 P.M. (10 P.M. IN SUMMER)

Price: Moderate
Credit cards: AE, MC, V
Wheelchair accessible except for bathrooms
No smoking
No alcohol

Satisfaction Feast is as friendly and inviting as the gentle aromas of fresh baking that waft through its dining room. The warm gold walls, vivid paintings, plants, and fresh flowers, along with meditative music, help to create a distinctively peaceful dining experience.

Satisfaction Feast is considered by many of Halifax's locals as the city's premier vegetarian restaurant. Delicious and nutritious vegan and nonvegan dishes are offered at reasonable prices.

Owner Sarita Earp describes the clientele as mixed. "It's a cross-range of people from vegetarians to meat-eaters who come here often because they love the delicious food that we serve."

Popular items on the menu include the delicious Tofini Sandwich (tofu spread with tahini, tamari, celery, onion and sprouts) and the Thali Plate (curry of the day, soup, yogurt, samosa, pappadam, pilau rice, and tomato chutney).

A wonderful cold beverage treat is the yogurt or soy milk smoothie, flavored with banana, strawberry, raspberry, mango, or rose.

Organically raised products are used for salads, and coffee made from organically grown coffee beans is served.

Gado Gado

Serves 6 as a main course

"Gado Gado is an Indonesian and vegan specialty that's very popular here," says owner Sarita Earp. "Indonesian and Thai food is very in right now, and this dish is always a sell-out."

2 to 4 tablespoons oil

2 cups sliced onions

$1/2$ tablespoon minced garlic

2 tablespoons grated fresh ginger

$1/2$ stalk fresh lemongrass, or $1/4$ teaspoon dried lemongrass

1 bay leaf

$1/2$ teaspoon green curry paste (optional)

4 cups sliced zucchini

4 cups broccoli florets

4 cups chopped Napa cabbage, or bok choy

$1 1/2$ cups chopped green bell pepper

$1/3$ bunch green onions, chopped

PEANUT SAUCE

$1^1/4$ cups natural peanut butter

1 tablespoon honey (optional)

$1/2$ teaspoon cayenne pepper and $1/2$ teaspoon ground ginger

$1^1/2$ tablespoons fresh or bottled lemon juice

1 tablespoon fresh or bottled lime juice

1 tablespoon cider vinegar

$1/2$ tablespoon rice wine vinegar (optional)

$3/4$ cup water

1 pound mung bean sprouts

$1/2$ cup raisins

Steamed brown rice or cooked rice stick (vermicelli) noodles, or other noodles for serving

In a medium skillet over medium heat, heat oil and sauté onions, garlic, ginger, bay leaf, and optional curry paste until onions are translucent. Steam zucchini, broccoli, cabbage or bok choy, peppers, and green onions until crisp-tender.

To make sauce: In a medium bowl, combine all ingredients and add to sautéed vegetables; simmer to blend flavors.

Combine sprouts, raisins, steamed and sautéed vegetables. Serve over brown rice or noodles.

THE GREEN DOOR RESTAURANT
198 Main Street
Ottawa, Ontario
K1S 1C6 Canada
613-234-9597

OPEN TUESDAY THROUGH SATURDAY 11 A.M. TO 9 P.M., SUNDAY UNTIL 3 P.M.

Price: Moderate
Credit cards: AE, MC, V
Wheelchair accessible with one small step up from street
No smoking
Alcohol: Beer and wine

Yes, the front door is green, much of the decor is green, and in fact, much of the food served here is green, for this restaurant serves one of the best vegetarian buffets in Ottawa.

A local favorite since 1988, the Green Door Restaurant is located in a quiet residential neighborhood one block east of the historic Rideau Canal, one block west of the Rideau River, and a mile from Parliament Hill and the heart of downtown Ottawa. Just across the street is a beautiful park adjoined by St. Paul University.

Owner Poppy Weaver describes the restaurant's atmosphere as relaxed and casual, and one that attracts a wide variety of clientele: "people of all ages and from all walks of life." Another drawing card is the art by local artists and schoolchildren that adorns the walls of this cafeteria-style restaurant.

The largely open kitchen is situated directly behind the buffet. Don't be surprised to see chefs dressed in tie-dyed T-shirts and groovy hats dashing out of the kitchen every so often to refill the buffet!

At the Green Door, organic flours are used to make tasty and popular sourdough breads. Yeast-free, wheat-free, and sugar- and honey-free baked goods are also available. Very few eggs or dairy products are utilized in food preparation, and the restaurant specializes in macrobiotic as well as organic dishes.

From the hot buffet, try Lentil Stew with Carrots, Mashed Potatoes with Kale, or the Polenta Casserole with Baked Beans and Parmesan Cheese — they are among the guests' favorites.

The cold buffet offers such delicious choices as Spicy Chickpea Salad, Marinated Beet Salad, Greek Salad, and an excellent guacamole. All the food is fresh and the buffets are replenished frequently.

Beers, wines, organic fruit juices, herbal teas, and filtered water are located near the cashier, where customers pay for their food by its weight. And don't forget the desserts. The dessert menu features a tantalizing selection of everything from homemade apple pie to gluten-free sesame-chocolate cake and soy-custard trifle.

Quinoa Tabbouleh

Serves 6 to 8 as a side dish

Poppy Weaver says of Quinoa Tabbouleh that "it is a delicious, wheat-free, and nutritious vegetarian recipe. It combines a South American grain with a Middle Eastern traditional dish to make a wonderful, tasty salad. The Green Door chefs suggest you serve it with a bowl of vegetable soup and a slice of whole-grain bread for a very satisfying lunch."

1 cup quinoa

2 cups water

1^1/2 teaspoons sea salt

^{1}/2 cup extra-virgin olive oil

^{1}/2 cup fresh lemon juice

2 small or 1 large garlic clove, crushed

^{1}/2 cup minced fresh mint leaves

2 cups finely chopped parsley

1 bunch green onions, including green portions, finely chopped

1 carrot, finely diced

^{1}/2 red bell pepper, seeded, deribbed, and diced

^{1}/2 green bell pepper, seeded, deribbed, and diced

Lettuce leaves, thin lemon slices, and black olives for serving

Wash and drain quinoa. In a medium saucepan, combine quinoa, water, and ^{1}/2 teaspoon salt. Bring to a boil. Reduce heat to a simmer, cover, and cook until all liquid is absorbed, 15 to 20 minutes.

Turn quinoa into a medium bowl and let cool completely.

Add remaining 1 teaspoon salt, olive oil, lemon juice, garlic, and mint to quinoa. Mix well. Add parsley, green onions, carrot, and bell peppers. Mix thoroughly, taste, and adjust seasoning. Line a platter with lettuce leaves, place salad on leaves, and garnish with lemon slices and black olives.

LE COMMENSAL
655 Bay Street
Toronto, Ontario
M5G 2K4 Canada
416-596-9364

OPEN DAILY 11:30 A.M. TO 10 P.M.

Price: Moderate
Credit Cards: AE, MC, V
Wheelchair accessible
No smoking
Alcohol: Wine and beer

This large, all-vegetarian buffet-style restaurant is a pleasant, peaceful respite on a busy big-city street.

Tastefully decorated in Southern French country style, Commensal, which means "table companion" in French, has won rave reviews from such publications as *Toronto Life Magazine* and *Living Naturally Magazine*, as well as from the Canadian Natural Health Association.

Founded in Montreal 20 years ago, the original restaurant has grown into a chain of nine restaurants throughout that city and the surrounding area. The Toronto establishment follows in the tradition of its Montreal predecessor.

Freshness and simplicity are the hallmarks of the food served here. All food is sold by weight — including salads — and food may be ordered to eat here or to take out.

There are daily lunch specials, and the fresh organic bread from the St. Lawrence market is especially recommended. Diners have more than one hundred different dishes to choose from, both hot and cold. Quench your thirst from the juice bar, which serves up delicious concoctions.

At Le Commensal you will also find a large variety of salads, many made with organic ingredients. The Marinated Avocado is especially yummy. Interesting salad dressings — including Avocado Vinaigrette — and toppings are available.

Some of the restaurant's most popular dishes are Ginger Tofu, Lasagna, Leek Potpie, Sweet Potatoes and Kasha, and Beet and Apple Salad. All dishes are marked as to whether they are vegan or contain milk and eggs.

An elaborate array of desserts is available, and they are all excellent — including Coffee Mousse Cake, Strawberry Shortcake, and the Bumbleberry Pie.

Even if you are not a vegetarian, this is a restaurant to check out while visiting Toronto. In fact, Le Commensal has discovered that 90 percent of its customers are not vegetarians, but people who love innovative, healthy food.

Ginger Tofu

Serves 2 as a main course

"This very popular dish is easy to make at home," says Le Commensal's manger, Susanna Yeung. "At the restaurant we marinate the organic tofu overnight and bake it the next day."

1 pound medium-firm organic tofu, cut into $1/2$-inch-thick slices
2 tablespoons fresh grated ginger
$1/4$ cup cold-pressed sunflower oil
$1/4$ cup tamari soy sauce
Minced shallots for garnish (optional)

Lay tofu slices in 1 layer in a shallow, nonreactive baking pan.

In a small bowl, combine ginger, oil, and soy sauce and mix until creamy. Pour evenly over tofu. Cover and refrigerate for about 12 hours.

Preheat oven to 350ºF. Bake tofu until golden, about 25 to 30 minutes. Avoid overcooking. Using a slotted spatula, lift tofu from pan and serve, sprinkled with shallots, if you like.

INDEX

U

New World Library is dedicated to
publishing books and cassettes that inspire
and challenge us to improve the quality
of our lives and our world.

For a catalog of our fine books
and cassettes, contact:

New World Library
14 Pamaron Way
Novato, CA 94949

Telephone: (415) 884-2100
Fax: (415) 884-2199
Or call toll-free (800) 972-6657
Catalog requests: Ext. 50
Ordering: Ext. 52

E-mail: escort@nwlib.com
http://www.nwlib.com